PLAY SONGS BEGINNING GUITAR

BY RON CENTOLA

To Jennifer and Mark

Edited by Anna H. Centola

TABLE OF CONTENTS

TABLE OF CONTENTS Cont.

TABLE OF CONTENTS Cont.

List Of Songs (Melodies)

List Of Songs (Rhythms)

INTRODUCTION

This method has been developed over ten years of teaching and research, using literally thousands of students at all ages. It is a completely effective self-taught method.

This book is filled with new ideas and methods that make learning music and guitar at home not only possible but enjoyable. These ideas and methods were developed around common questions that have confused students trying to learn the guitar. You will find your questions anticipated and answered.

Professional guitar teachers may use this method as a basic and systematic approach from which creative and supplemental material may be added to stimulate interest. This method does not deny that a teacher may add much to bring the student beyond the reaches or intent of this book.

I sincerely hope that this book opens the door of music to those of all ages.

Ron Centola

SPECIAL FEATURES

1) You don't need to know anything about music.

2) There is a section on how to check your old guitar to see if it is playable. Also, there is a section on buying a new or used guitar.

3) There are special "tear out" aids to help you play songs. These aids will save you the time and frustration of constantly having to flip back through pages to find what you have learned.

4) Instructions are set out in a point by point form.

5) There are plenty of opportunities to reinforce what you have learned with practice aids consisting of common, traditional songs that most people are familiar with.

6) Songs are written twice: once with symbol coded, new notes which have the counting marked in, and once in standard music.

7) Important points to remember are in bold print.

8) There is a special section on how to accompany another person playing the guitar or any other musical instrument.

PREPARATION TO PLAY

1) A. *DOES IT MATTER IF YOU ARE RIGHT OR LEFT-HANDED?*
   B. *DOES THE GUITAR HAVE TO BE STRUNG A SPECIAL WAY IF YOU ARE LEFT-HANDED?*

   A. NO — Since you are going to use both hands to play the guitar, it doesn't matter whether you are right or left-handed.
   B. NO — Since all diagrams are made for standard strung guitars, you are making things very difficult for yourself if you have the guitar restrung.

2) *SHOULD YOUR NAILS BE TRIMMED?*

   YES — Your nails should not extend beyond your finger tips. If your nails are too long, you will not be able to play the guitar clearly.

3) *DOES IT MATTER IF YOU HAVE STEEL OR NYLON STRINGS?*

   NO — Steel or nylon strings are merely for sound preference. However, it is true that nylon strings will be easier on your fingers. With steel strings your fingers will hurt until you build up a callus on the tips of your fingers.

4) *DOES IT MATTER IF YOU HAVE AN ELECTRIC OR ACOUSTIC GUITAR? (ACOUSTIC IS A NON-ELECTRIC GUITAR)*

   NO — You play the electric and acoustic guitar the same way. The difference is that an electric guitar is louder (if an amplifier is used) and is probably easier to play because you don't have to press down on the strings as hard to produce a sound.

5) *CAN YOU USE THE OLD GUITAR THAT HAS BEEN LYING AROUND THE HOUSE FOR YEARS?*

   Look on the following pages in CHECK YOUR GUITAR to see if it is playable.

6) *DO YOU HAVE TO BE MUSICALLY INCLINED TO PLAY THE GUITAR?*

NO — It helps, but it is not necessary. Anyone who is willing to practice can play the guitar or any other instrument.

7) *DO YOU NEED A PICK?*

You may want to use a pick. I feel that it is better to use your thumb because you have a better feel of the strings. I refer to striking the strings with your thumb, but you may use a pick instead.

PARTS OF YOUR GUITAR

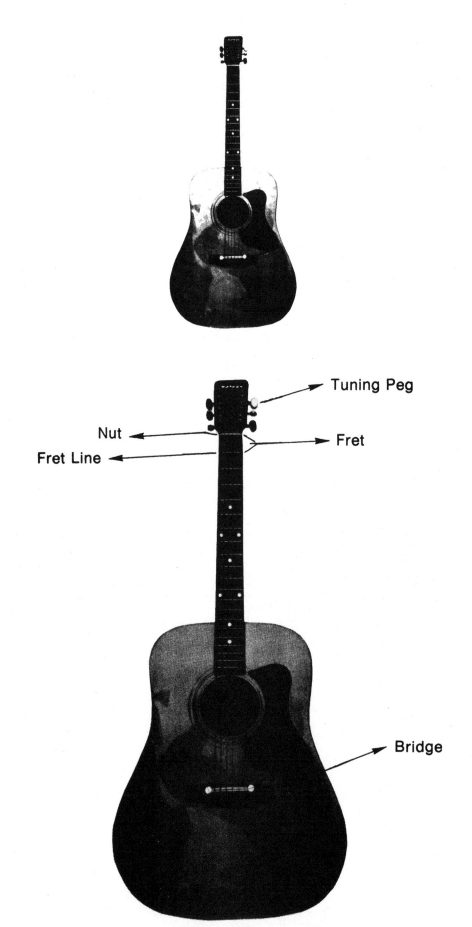

CHECK YOUR GUITAR

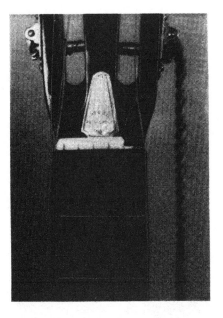

1) Check the top of the guitar (the nut) to see if it is **cracked** or broken.

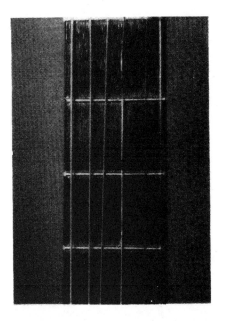

2) Check for frayed **or split** strings. This will **cause thuds** (unclear sounds).

3) Check for a collapsed **bridge**.

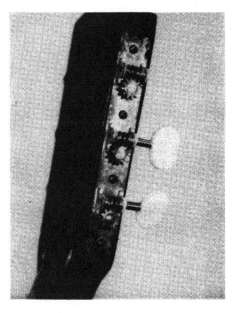

4) Check for broken tuning **pegs**. If they are broken, you **cannot** tune the guitar.

1, 2, 3, 4 are inexpensive **repairs** that any music store could **correct**.

CHECK YOUR GUITAR

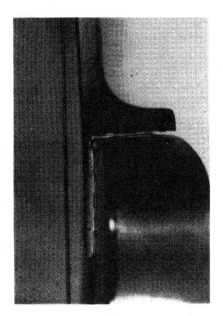

5) Check that the neck is not separated from the body of the guitar.

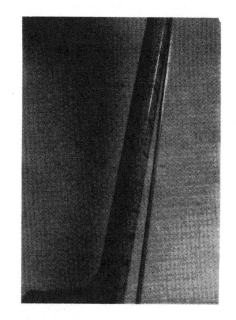

6) Check that the body of the guitar is not warped. If it is warped, the strings will be too far away from the neck to play.

5 and 6 are major repairs. If the guitar is old and inexpensive, you would be better off getting a new guitar.

STUDENT NOTES

HOW TO HOLD THE GUITAR

HOW TO HOLD A PICK

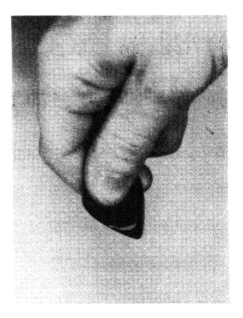

HOW YOUR FINGERS ARE NUMBERED

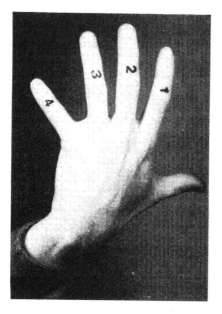

The numbering of your fingers may seem simple, but it is extremely important. Study this photo closely and remember this numbering of your fingers.

HOW TO READ A GUITAR DIAGRAM

FULL GUITAR

THE NECK OF GUITAR

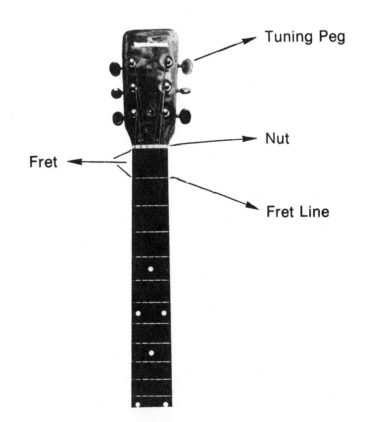

GUITAR DIAGRAM

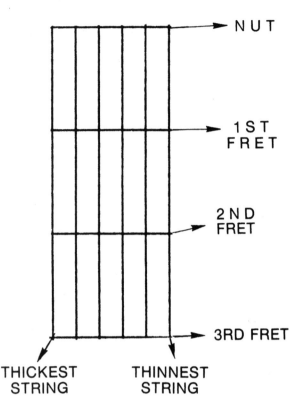

This diagram will be used throughout the book to show finger positions on the guitar.

HOW TO READ FINGER POSITIONS ON THE GUITAR DIAGRAM

O indicates finger placed on guitar. The number in the circle would be the number of the finger used on your hand.

② indicates the 2nd finger on the 2nd fret of the 3rd string.

③ indicates the 3rd finger on the 3rd fret of the 5th string.

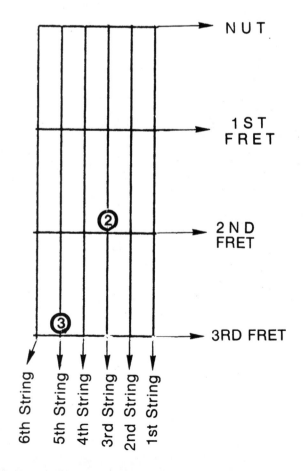

BASIC ELEMENTS OF MUSIC

Most of the elements of music that you need to know will be learned while actually playing the guitar. Here are some things that you should be familiar with in order to start.

1) Music for guitar, as well as any other instrument, will be placed on a **staff** which consists of **5 lines** and **4 spaces.**

    A. THESE **are not** STRINGS OF THE GUITAR.

    B. A way to remember the lines of the staff is by using the sentence **E**very **G**ood **B**oy **D**oes **F**ine. The first letter of each word indicates the name of the line. The spaces may be remembered easily since they spell "Face."

2)

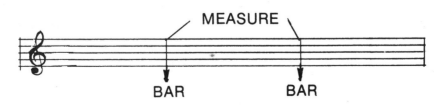

    A. The **bars** are a way of dividing the staff into segments called measures. **A measure is the space between two bars.**

BASIC ELEMENTS OF MUSIC (Contd.)

3)  G CLEF

This is a **G Clef** . All music written for guitar will be preceded by the clef sign.

4) TIME SIGNATURES

A. The G Clef will be found at the very beginning of each line.

B. The **time signature** will only be found at the very beginning of the song, next to the G Clef . It is not found on the following lines of the song.

C.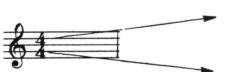

This number indicates there are 4 beats per measure.

This number indicates the type of note that receives one beat. (a quarter note receives one beat in all the above time signatures).

D.

Most songs are written in $\frac{4}{4}$ time. Since $\frac{4}{4}$ is the most common time used, a C is often used instead of the $\frac{4}{4}$. The meaning, however, is the same.

BASIC ELEMENTS OF MUSIC (Contd.)

5) NOTES

   A. Notes are a way of communicating musical language, as words are a way of communicating spoken language. You will learn to translate the notes from the musical staff and apply them to the guitar. This will be one of the main objects of this book.

   B. Notes have 3 basic forms: o , ♩ , ♩

   C. **The note takes the name of the line or space upon which it is placed on the musical staff.**

This note is a G because it is on the G line of the staff.

This note is a C because it is on the C space of the staff.

6) MUSICAL ALPHABET

   A. The musical alphabet is limited to 7 letters.
   A, B, C, D, E, F and G. In the musical alphabet these 7 letters repeat themselves for a great deal of variation in notes. A, B, C, D, E, F, G, A, B, C ETC.

7) **It doesn't matter which way the stem of the note is going.**

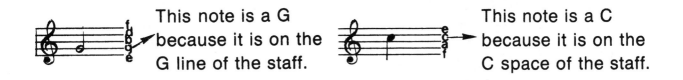

stem → ♩ ♩ . The direction of the stem does not affect the name or value of the note.

8) ARE YOU CONFUSED?

   A. You should be. All of these things will come together as you actually play the guitar. **This section is here for a reference and does not have to be memorized.**

THE FIRST POSITION

PREPARATION TO PLAY   PUTTING YOUR FINGERS DOWN

1) Before and while playing any exercise on the guitar, you should put your hand in the first position.

2) The purpose of putting your **left hand** in the **first position** is to avoid looking at your hand. When you begin to play you must look at the music and not your hand.

3) Place your hand in the first position.

4) This is a practice for your left hand. **you should not be striking the guitar with your right hand.**

5) **FINGER AND FRET** — If your hand is in the correct position, when you put down your **1st finger** you should be on the **1st fret**. (At this point it doesn't matter what string you are on, as long as you are on the first fret). When you put down your **2nd finger** you should be on the **2ND Fret**. When you put down your **3rd finger** you should be on the **3rd fret.**

6) As you can see (Putting Your Fingers Down Photo), when you put your fingers down your thumb will move to the back center of the guitar.

YOU ARE NOW READY TO PLAY THE GUITAR
(THE NOTES ON THE FIRST STRING)

1) **Remember, before you begin playing, place your left hand in the first position.**

2) You are now ready to play the first note on your guitar. The first note you are going to play is E.

 Any note placed in this space of the musical staff is E.

3) **All three of these E's are played the same way but are counted differently.**

4) To play E you strike the first string with the thumb of your right hand. You strike the string directly over the hole of your guitar. Your left hand should remain in the first position without placing any fingers down on the neck. **Striking the string with the thumb of your right hand without placing any fingers of your left hand down is called playing the string open.**

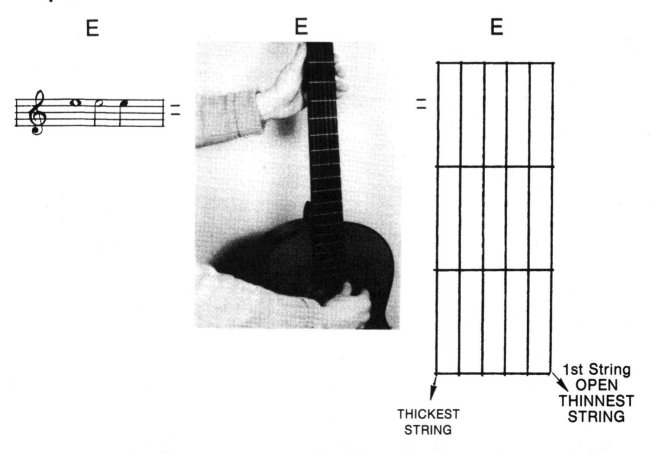

E   E   E

THICKEST STRING

1st String OPEN THINNEST STRING

HOW TO COUNT THE THREE KINDS OF E's

WHOLE NOTE o

1)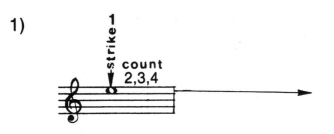

This E IS A WHOLE NOTE. All whole notes are worth 4 beats.

2) o = **WHOLE NOTE**   o = **4 BEATS**

STRIKE NOTE	= **1 BEAT**
+ COUNT	= **3 BEATS**
o =	**4 BEATS**

3) You strike the E, or 1st string, open (no fingers down) and then you **count 2, 3, 4 after you strike the note. Striking the note is the first beat.**

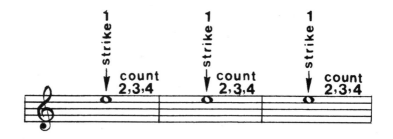

4) Strike the E and count 2, 3, 4. Repeat. **Do not look at your thumb** while you are playing this exercise. Look at the music and try to remember what E looks like. **Count evenly. Do not race your count.** Your left hand should be in the 1st position.

HALF-NOTE

1)

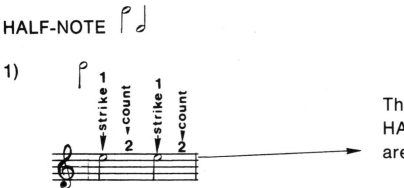

This is also an E. This E is a HALF NOTE. All half notes are worth 2 beats.

It doesn't matter which way the stem of the note is going. ♩ ♩ ♩ ♩. The direction of the stem does not affect the name or value of the note.

HOW TO COUNT THE THREE KINDS OF E's

2) ♩ = **HALF NOTE**   ♩ = **2 BEATS**   **STRIKE NOTE** = **1 BEAT**

3) You strike the E, or 1st string, open (no fingers down) and then you count 2 after you strike the note. Striking the note is the first beat.

COUNTING

4) Strike the E and count 2 after you play each note. Do not look at your thumb. Count evenly.

QUARTER-NOTE

1)   Strike each note — do not count between notes

2) = **QUARTER NOTE**   ♩ = **1 BEAT**   **STRIKE NOTE** = **1 BEAT**

3) You strike the E, or 1st string, open (no fingers down). **You proceed from note to note without counting in between.**

4) Do not look at your thumb. Your left hand should be in the 1st position.

COMBINATION EXERCISE

SUMMARY

1) Your hand should be in the 1st position.

2) You should not look at your thumb.

3) Keep your eyes on the music.

4) You play the above E's the same way on the guitar, though the number of beats they are worth vary, depending on how they look.

5) Keep your count even and smooth.

6) Count after you strike the note.

THE F NOTE

1) 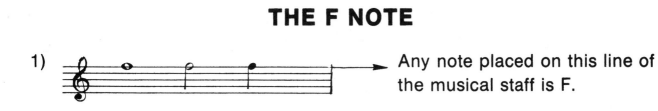 Any note placed on this line of the musical staff is F.

2) All F's on this line are played the same way, although they may be counted differently.

3) To play **F** you put your **1st finger** of your left hand on the **1st fret** (right above the fret line) of the **1st string.** Now strike the 1st string with the thumb of your right hand.

4)

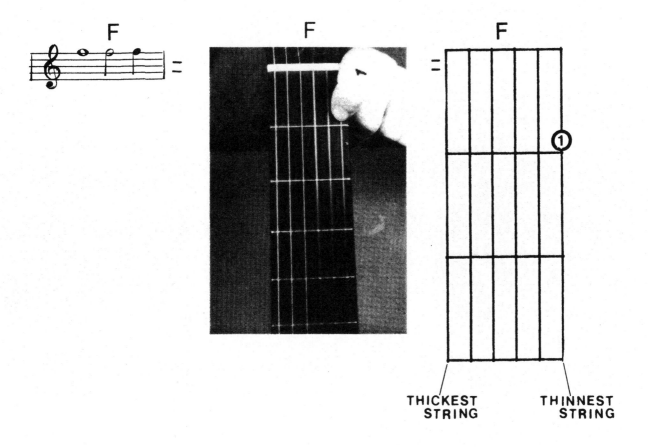

THICKEST STRING   THINNEST STRING

GETTING RID OF THE THUD

DID YOU THUD (YOU ARE NOT GETTING A CLEAR SOUND) WHEN YOU PLAYED F? CHECK THESE POINTS BELOW CAREFULLY.

To get a clear sound you must observe the following points.

1) **Press with the tip of your finger.** If your nails are not trimmed evenly with your finger tips, you will not be able to get a clear sound.

2) Press your thumb on the back center of the guitar. Your thumb and 1st finger can be used as a vise. The harder you press your thumb, the more pressure you will be putting on your 1st finger.

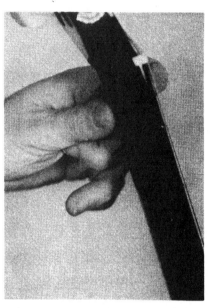

3) **Press firmly.**

4) Do not release the pressure from your 1st finger as you strike the string with your thumb.

5) Put your 1st finger right above the fret line. **Your finger should not be on the fret line.** (Check the page in the book on Parts Of The Guitar).

ANY ONE OF THESE, OR ANY COMBINATION OF THESE POINTS, WILL CAUSE A THUD.

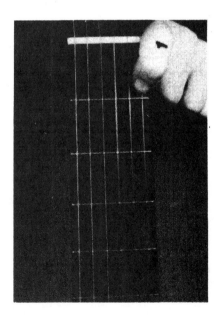

DOES YOUR FINGER HURT?

Your fingers may hurt for a few days, especially if you have steel strings. After a few days of practice, you will develop calluses on your fingers and they will not hurt any more. In other words, the best remedy for "finger hurt" is practice.

ARE YOU USING THE RULE OF KEEPING YOUR HAND IN THE FIRST POSITION?

Before you play F, your hand should be in the 1st position. If your hand is in the proper position, you should be able to put your 1st finger on F without looking at your left hand or the thumb of your right hand. If you get used to looking at your hands, you will not be able to look at the music.

PLAY THIS EXERCISE WITHOUT LOOKING AT YOUR FINGERS.

STUDENT'S NOTES
(Use this space to write down any important points that you want to remember).

COMBINATION EXERCISE E AND F

1) These exercises are not any particular song or tune.

2) **The same exercise is written twice.** One has the counting marked in and the other doesn't. The purpose of this is to check yourself to see if you know the values of the various notes.

3) You should be able to play the F clearly.

4) You should not have to look at your fingers.

5) You should know your note values.

EXERCISE

THE G NOTE

1)

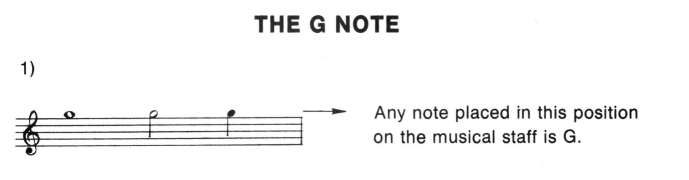

Any note placed in this position on the musical staff is G.

2) All G's placed in this position on the musical staff are played the same way, although they may be counted differently.

3) To play **G** you place the **3rd finger** of your left hand on the **3rd fret** (right above the fret line) of the **1st string.** Now strike the 1st string with the thumb of your right hand.

4)

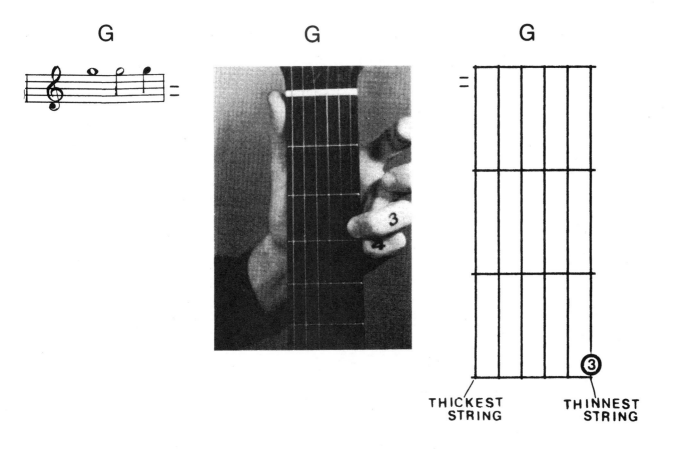

G   G   G

THICKEST STRING   THINNEST STRING

COMBINATION E, F, AND G

1) Use the 1st position. Remember, when you put down your 1st finger you should be on the 1st fret. When you put down your 3rd finger you should be on the 3rd fret. **Look at the music and not your fingers.**

2) Do you know your note values? Can you play the 2nd version of the song without looking at the counting?

3) Can you play F and G without thudding?

4) Do you recognize E, F, and G as whole notes, half-notes, and quarter-notes?

EXERCISE

INTRODUCTION TO CHORDS

1) The same diagram that is used for the notes is also used for the chords.

2) A chord, however, is a combination of strings being played at the same time. The diagrams will show you which strings to play and which strings not to play. **An X will be placed over the strings which should not be played.** The strings not marked should be played.

EXAMPLE

These two strings would not be played.

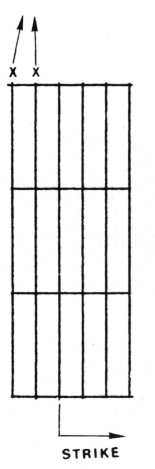

STRIKE

In this example, the 5th and 6th strings would not be played. The 4th, 3rd, 2nd, and 1st strings would be played (in that order). You would brush these 4 strings. **When you strum a chord you do not play the strings one at a time.** Your thumb (right hand) should brush evenly over these four strings.

CHORDS

1) A chord is any combination of notes. **When you strike a chord you will be playing more than one string.**

2) The first chord you are going to play is G. To play **G** you are going to put your **3rd finger** on the **3rd fret** of the **1st string**. This is the G note that you learned in your 1st lesson. However, for this note to become a G CHORD **you must also strike the 4th, 3rd, and 2nd strings open.**

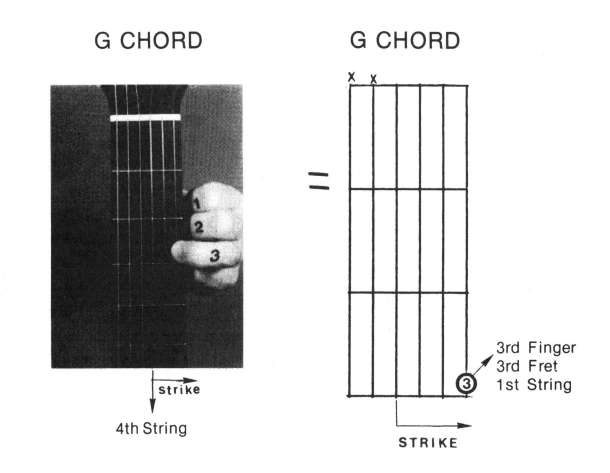

G CHORD   G CHORD

strike

4th String

3rd Finger
3rd Fret
1st String

STRIKE

3) To play G you strike strings 4, 3, 2, and 1 evenly with the thumb of your right hand. You do not play the strings one at a time but, instead, you brush all 4 strings down evenly.

4) Play the G chord 4 times — EVENLY.

THE G SEVENTH (G^7) CHORD

1) To play the G^7 chord you are also going to play the 1st four strings. To play **G^7** you are going to put your **1st finger** on the **1st fret** on the **1st string**. This is the F note that you learned on the 1st string. However, for the note to become a G^7 chord, you must also add the 4th, 3rd, and 2nd strings open. These 3 strings open, plus the F note, form the G^7 chord.

G^7 CHORD   G^7 CHORD

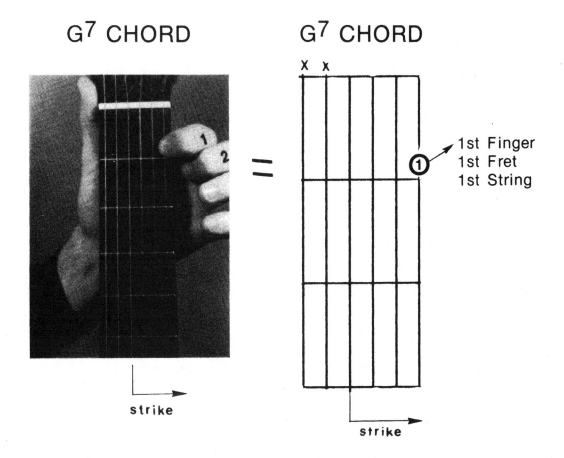

1st Finger
1st Fret
1st String

strike

strike

2) To play G^7 strike the 4TH, 3RD, 2ND, and 1ST STRINGS evenly with your thumb or pick.

3) Play the G^7 chord 4 times evenly and without stopping.

4) When playing a chord make sure you keep your fingers up straight. (Right Hand)

COMBINATION G AND G⁷ CHORDS

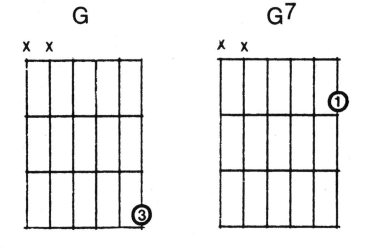

Listen to the first part of the record on chords.

Do not stop between chord changes.

1) Strike the chord 1 time for each **|** . You will play G 4 times (**||||**) and the G⁷ 4 times (**||||**) and proceed.

2) Your hand should be in the 1st position when you play this or any exercise. If your hand is in the 1st position, when you put down your 1st finger you should be on the 1st fret. Also, when you put down your 3rd finger you should be on the 3rd fret.

3) You should be playing the strings evenly and clearly.

4) **You should not stop between chords. You do this by keeping your strumming hand (right hand) going.** This is difficult because if you get confused with your left hand, your right hand will stop. **Force your strumming hand to keep going while you are changing from G to G⁷.**

5) Play only 4 strings.

6) Do not look at your hands.

THE NOTES ON YOUR SECOND STRING — THE B NOTE

1)

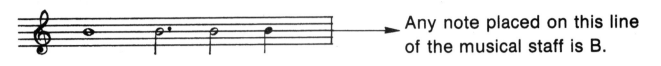

→ Any note placed on this line of the musical staff is B.

2) All of these B's are played the same way. You should count the whole note, half note, and quarter note in the same way as you did for E.

The dotted half note will be explained on page 31.

3) To play **B** you strike the **2nd string open** (no fingers down) with the thumb of your right hand. Your left hand should be in the first position.

4)   B   B   B

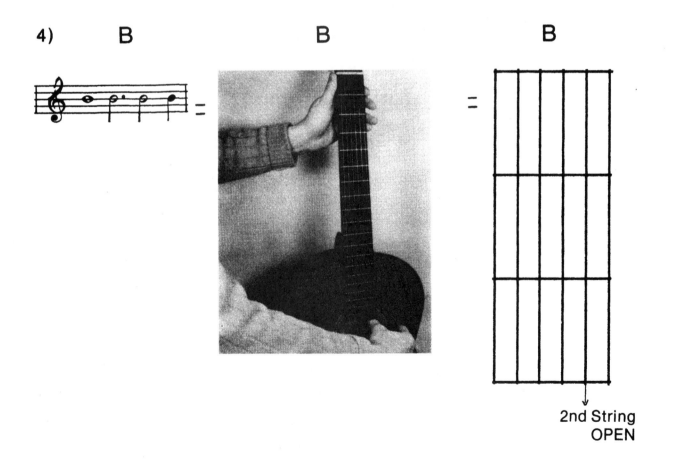

2nd String
OPEN

THUMB-TO-STRING

1) Because you are playing the 2nd string, you are going to be tempted to look at the thumb of your right hand.

2) The thumb-to-string method eliminates the necessity of looking at your right hand.

3) Thumb-to-string means that after you strike the string with your thumb or pick, your thumb should stop and rest on the string below. The string below acts as a backstop for your thumb. By using this method, you can feel where the string is that you are playing without having to look at your right hand.

4) Let's use thumb-to-string using the 2nd string as an example. After you strike B, or the 2nd string open, your thumb should rest on the 1st string. you do not play the 1st string. The 1st string acts as a backstop.

5) You will use thumb-to-string on all the strings that you play. When you play the 3rd string your thumb should stop on the 2nd string. When you play the 4th string your thumb should stop on the 3rd string, etc.

STUDENT'S NOTES

HOW TO COUNT A DOTTED HALF NOTE

1)

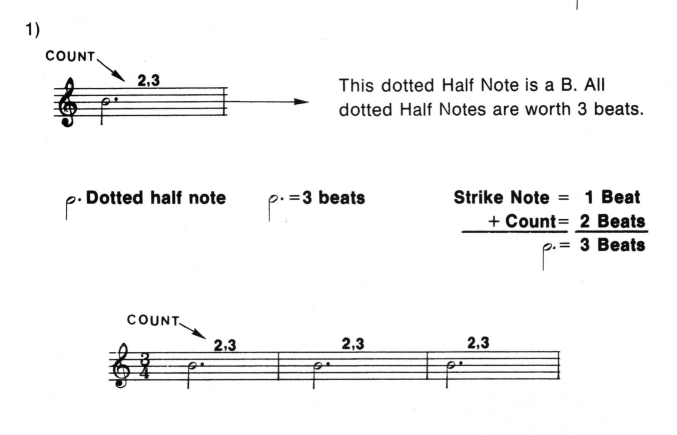

COUNT 2,3

This dotted Half Note is a B. All dotted Half Notes are worth 3 beats.

Dotted half note   **=3 beats**

Strike Note = 1 Beat
+ Count = 2 Beats
= 3 Beats

COUNT 2,3   2,3   2,3

EXERCISE IN B

1) Use thumb-to-string.
2) Keep your left hand in the first position.
3) Look at the music.

EXERCISE

THE C NOTE

1)  Any note placed on this **space** of the musical staff is C.

2) All these C's are played the same way, although each must be counted differently depending on the type of note they are. (Whole note, dotted half note, half note, quarter note)

3) To play **C** you put your **1st finger** on the **1st fret** of the **2nd string.** Remember, use your thumb-to-string method. After you strike C, your thumb should stop on the 1st string.

4)

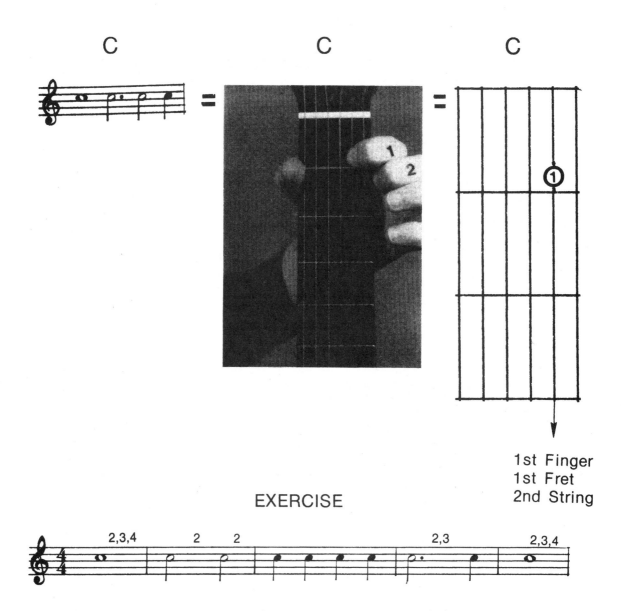

C   =   C   =   C

1st Finger
1st Fret
2nd String

EXERCISE

COMBINATION EXERCISE B AND C

1) Keep your left hand in the 1st position.

2) Use thumb-to-string with your right hand.

3) Look at the music.

4) Try to play the 2nd version without the counting marked in.

EXERCISE

THE D NOTE

1)

Any note placed on this line of the musical staff is D.

2) To play **D** you put your **3rd finger** on the **3rd fret** of the **2nd string.** Keep your hand in the 1st position and use your thumb-to-string method.

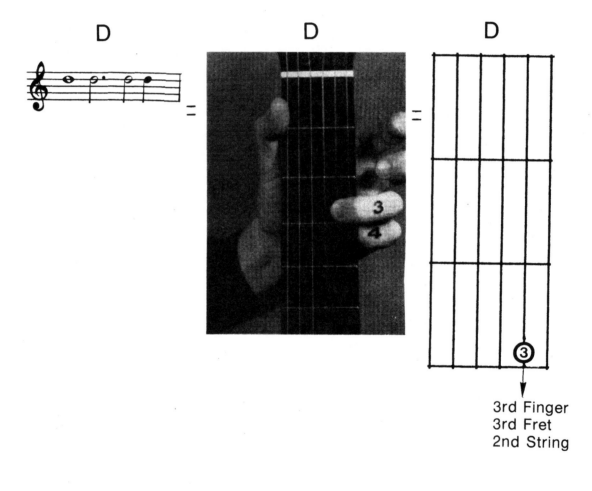

3rd Finger
3rd Fret
2nd String

EXERCISE

USING THE SYMBOL CODED NOTE CHART

1) You may tear out the symbol coded note chart on the perforated edge and place it next to the various tunes. When you are through using the symbol coded note chart you may place it in the pocket in the back of this book to protect against loss.

2) **Each song is written twice.** The first version is symbol coded according to what string the note is on, and has the timing written in. The second version is the exact same tune without the aids.

3) The four tunes are very familiar tunes. **Remember to keep your hand in the 1st position and use the thumb-to-string rules.** Look at the music and not your hands. Since the tunes are familiar, if you make a mistake you will hear it. You don't have to look to see if you are playing the correct notes. You can hear if you make a mistake. **Do not memorize where your fingers go in order to play a tune.**

4) When you can play all four songs in the unaided version you may proceed to the next string.

5) In all of these songs you can hear the basic tune but there are extra notes added to give them variety. Many times people will play tunes and feel that this or that note doesn't belong. These extra notes do however give the tunes a little bounce and if played correctly will make the songs in this book more enjoyable.

STUDENT'S NOTES

SYMBOL CODED NOTE CHART

FIRST STRING NOTES E, F, G

These notes will be
enclosed in a circle.

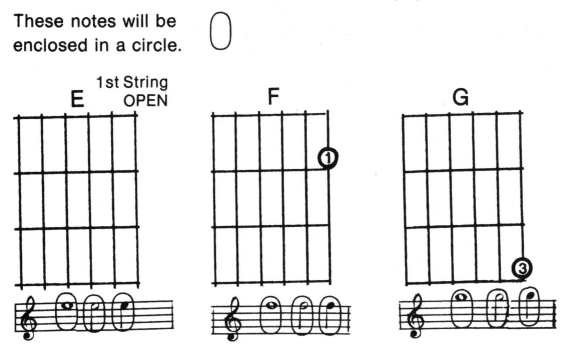

SECOND STRING NOTES B, C, D

These notes will be
enclosed in a rectangle.

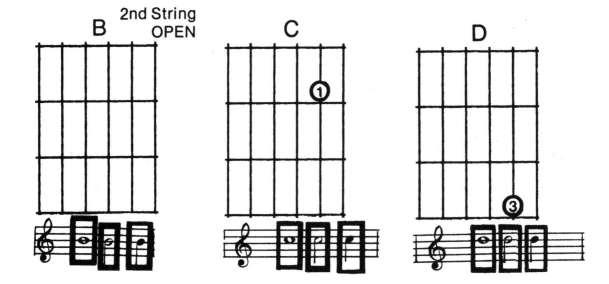

Tear or cut out on perforated edge. Place in the envelope on the back cover to protect against loss.

OH, DEAR, WHAT CAN THE MATTER BE

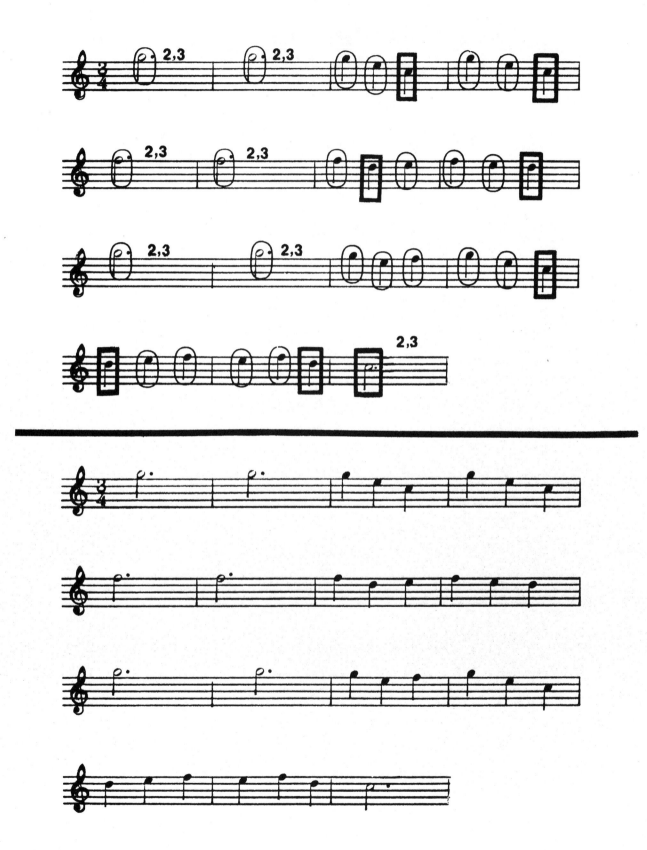

POP GOES THE WEASEL

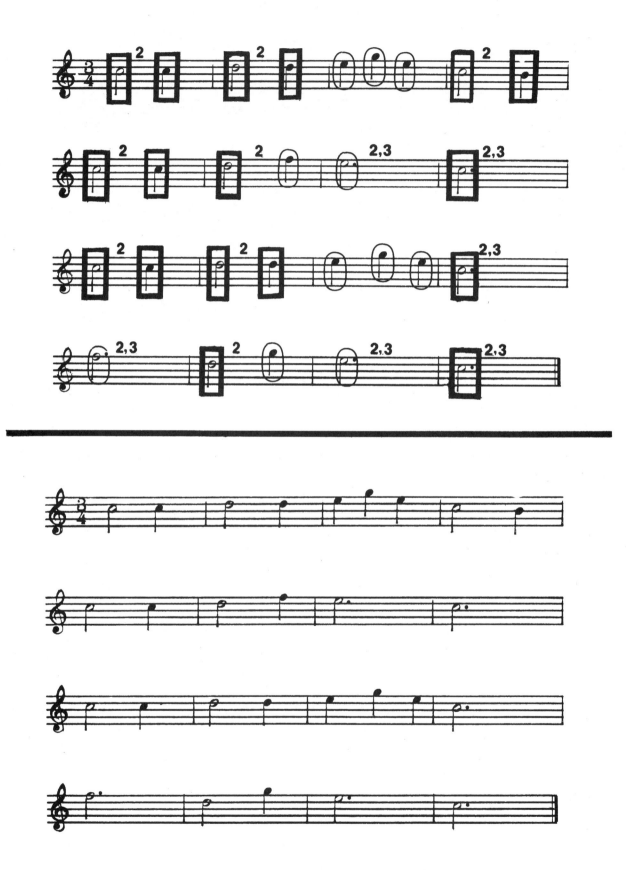

HERE WE GO ROUND THE MULBERRY BUSH

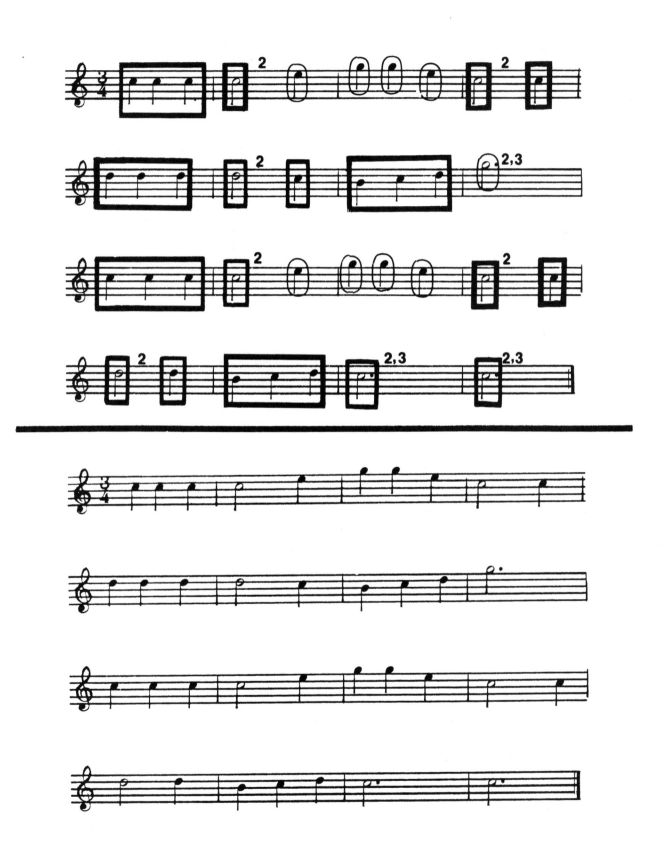

A-TISKET A-TASKET

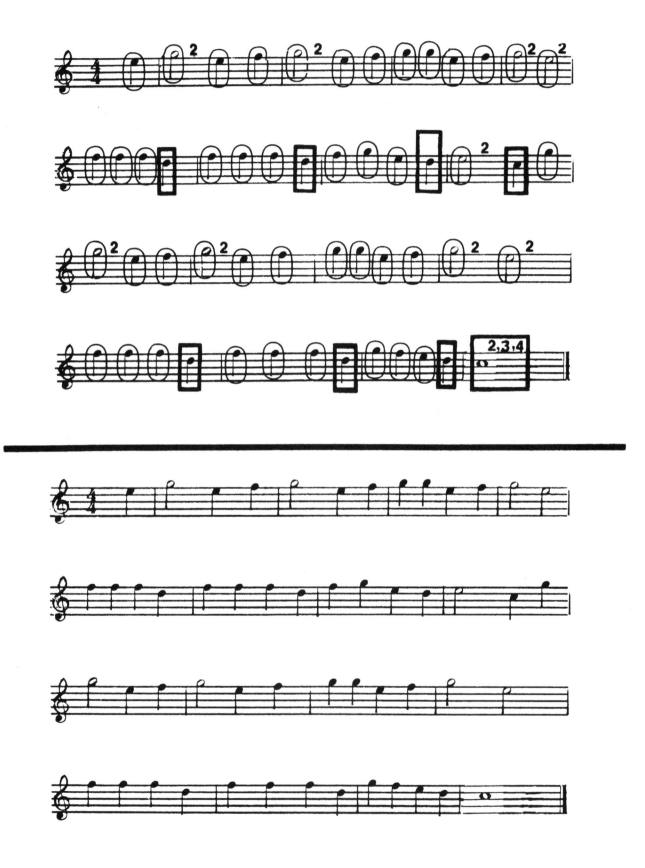

CHORDS AGAIN

THE C CHORD

1) To play **C** you place your **1st finger** on the **1st fret** of the **2nd string.** You place your **2nd finger** on the **2nd fret** of the **4th string.** You play strings 4, 3, 2, 1.

C — THE RIGHT WAY

Both of your fingers are up straight. If you bend your fingers over, as in photo (C THE WRONG WAY) your fingers will touch other strings and cause thuds. **Turn your left wrist counter-clockwise and your fingers will become straight.**

2) Press both fingers down at the same time.

3) When you place your fingers on C you are probably putting one finger down at a time (First finger down, then second finger down). **Try placing both fingers (1st and 2nd) down on the C chord at the same time.**

4) Keeping your hand in the first position, try placing both fingers on C without looking at your hand. Practice until you can do this.

THE C CHORD

C THE RIGHT WAY   C   C THE WRONG WAY

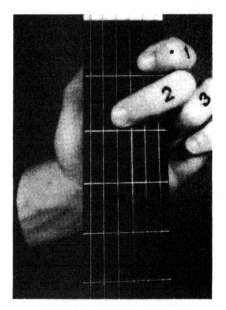

FLOW CHARTS

1) The flow chart is a means of showing you how to move from one chord to another with as little effort as possible. **The less you move your fingers around, the smoother and quicker you will be able to change from one chord to another.** The chord positions on the diagrams can be identified by rectangles and circles. The finger positions of the first chord will be enclosed in rectangles and the second, in circles.

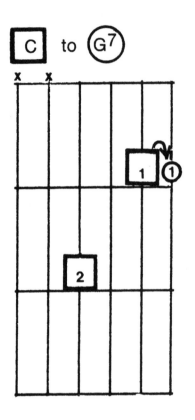

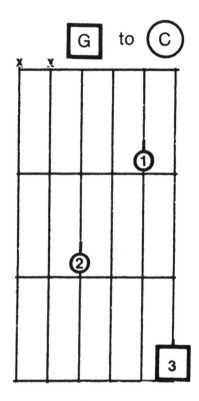

To change from C to G⁷ you must move your 1st finger from the 1st fret 2nd string to the 1st fret of the 1st string. Lift up your 2nd finger. To change from G⁷ to C reverse the entire process.

To change from G to C you must lift up your 3rd finger and place your 1st and 2nd fingers down as shown on the diagram.

HOW TO PLAY THE FOLLOWING SONGS USING CHORDS

1) There follow six common tunes. These tunes have only the words and the chords marked in.

2) To play these tunes you must sing the tunes and play the chords while singing. (It doesn't matter how bad your voice is. You are doing this to practice your chord changing).

3) There are no marks to indicate how many times you play each chord. This is done to avoid confusion. You merely play the chords with down strums and change chords when you see the chord change on top of the words.

4) You don't have to worry about how many times you must strike the chord. Your only concern is changing from one chord to another without stopping.

5) If you are confused as to where to place your left hand for C, G^7, or G, your right hand (strumming hand) will stop moving. It is important that you know where G^7, C, and G are without looking at your hands.

6) When you are playing these exercises **keep your strumming hand going through the chord changes.** Do not stop your strumming hand as you change from one chord to another.

STUDENT'S NOTES

MARY HAD A LITTLE LAMB

C ➡   **G**⁷ ➡

Mary had a little lamb, little lamb,

C ➡

little lamb, Mary had a little lamb, whose

G ➡   **C** ➡

fleece was white as snow.

WHERE HAS MY LITTLE DOG GONE?

C ➡   **G** ➡

Where, oh where has my   lit-tle dog gone,   oh where, oh where can he

C ➡   **G**⁷ ➡

be?   With his ears so long and his tail so short, oh where, oh where

C ➡

can he be?

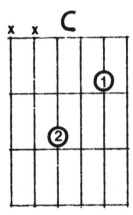

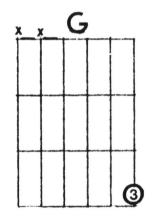

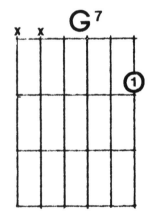

LA CUCARACHA

C ➡   **G** ➡

La Cu - ca - ra - cha, La Cu - ca - ra - cha, Does - n't want to travel far   La

C ➡

Cu - ca ra - cha, La Cu - ca - ra -cha, It does - n't have an old gui - tar, La

Cu - cu - ca ra - cha, La Cu - ca - ra - cha, La Cu - ca - ra - cha, Does - n't

G⁷ ➡   **G**⁷ ➡

want to travel far,   La Cu - ca - ra - cha, La Cu - ca - ra - cha, Never

C ➡

with an old gui - tar.

SHORTNIN' BREAD

C →
Three lit-tle child-ren, ly-ing in bed;   **G⁷** →
Two were sick and the oth-er

C →
most dead!

Sent for the doc-tor,   doc-tor said,   "Feed these chil-dren on

G⁷ → **C** →
short-nin' bread."

Ma-ma's lit-tle ba-by loves short-nin', short-nin',

G →   **C** →
Ma-ma's lit-tle ba-by loves short-nin' bread.

Ma-ma's lit-tle ba-by loves short-nin',   Ma-ma's lit-tle ba-by loves

G → **C** →
short-nin' bread.

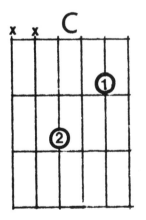
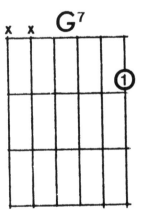
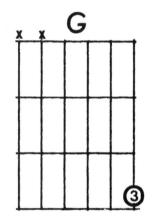

WHEN THE SAINTS GO MARCHING IN

C →
Oh,   when the saints   go march-ing in,

G⁷ →
Oh,   when the saints go march-ing in,

C →   **G** →
Oh, Lord, I want to be in the num-ber

C → **G⁷** → **C** →
When the saints go march-ing in.

SHOO, FLY, DON'T BOTHER ME

C➡   G⁷➡   C➡

Shoo, fly, don't both-er me, Shoo, fly, don't both-er me, Shoo, fly, don't

G⁷➡   C➡

both-er me, For I be-long to company G.

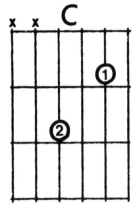
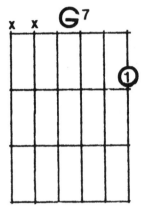
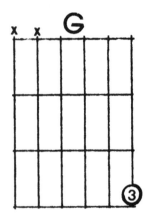

SKIP TO MY LOU

C➡   G⁷➡   C➡

Skip, skip, skip to my Lou, skip, skip, skip to my Lou, skip, skip, skip to my

G➡   C➡

Lou, skip to my Lou my dar-ling.

A TISKET, A TASKET

C➡   G⁷➡

A tisket, a tasket, a green and yellow basket, My mommy sent me with a

G➡   C➡

letter, and on the way I lost it.

THE NOTES ON THE THIRD STRING

1) 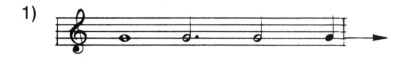 Any note placed on this line of the musical staff is G

2) To play **G** you play the **3rd string open.** (no fingers down)

3) Although this G and the G you learned on the 1st string, have the same name, you can tell them apart by looking at them.

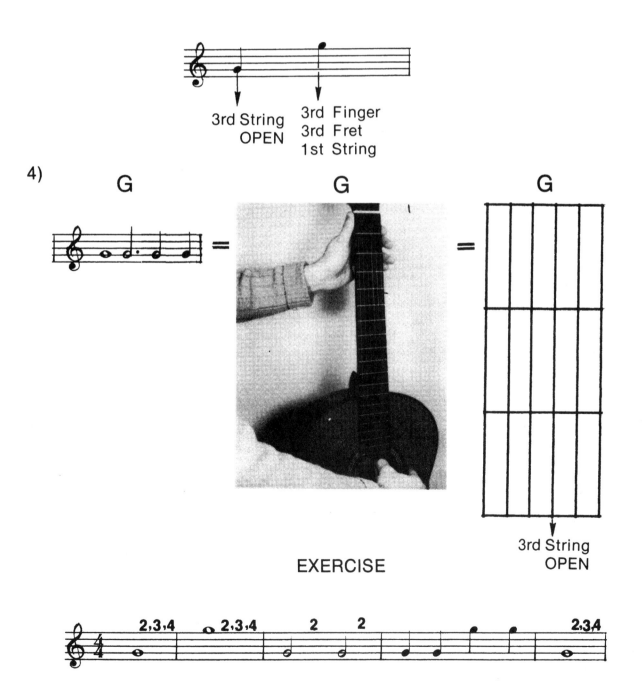

3rd String OPEN   3rd Finger 3rd Fret 1st String

4)   G   G   G

3rd String OPEN

EXERCISE

THE G's AND A TIE

1) A tie is when one note is connected to another note with a looped line.

2) It does not matter whether the tie is on the top or the bottom of the note.

3) When one note is tied to another note you do not play the second note. Notes that are tied will always be the same notes. When one note is tied to another you **play the 1st note and count its value (whole note, half note etc.). Then, you continue to hold the 1st note and count the total value of the 2nd note.** You count the total value of the 2nd note because you are not playing it.

X Indicates that you do not play that note but count its value.

EXERCISE

Count 2,3,4 after you strike this note — let the note ring as you count the tie.

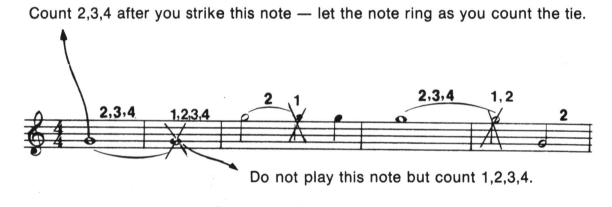

Do not play this note but count 1,2,3,4.

THE A

1)  Any note in this space of the musical staff is A.

2) To play **A** you put your 2nd finger on the **2nd fret** of the **3rd string.**

3)

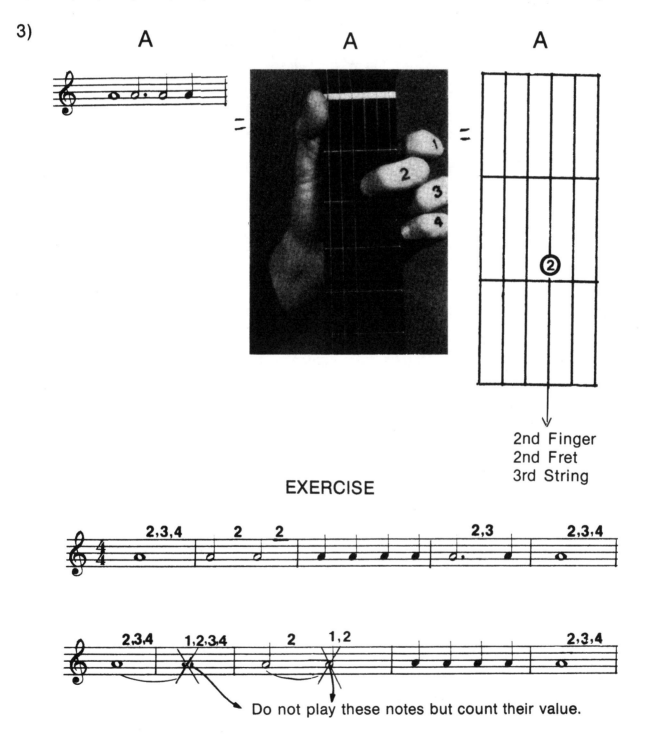

2nd Finger
2nd Fret
3rd String

EXERCISE

Do not play these notes but count their value.

RESTS

1) **A rest in music is a period of silence.** When you see a rest you count the number of beats it is worth, although you do not play anything. A rest is a pause in the music for a certain number of beats.

1 BEAT   2 BEATS   4 BEATS

RESTS (WITH G AND A ON THE THIRD STRING)

EXERCISE

Count the value of the note — Then count the value of the rest.

Do not hold the note while you count the rest. A rest is a period of silence.

SYMBOL CODED NOTE CHART

2ND STRING

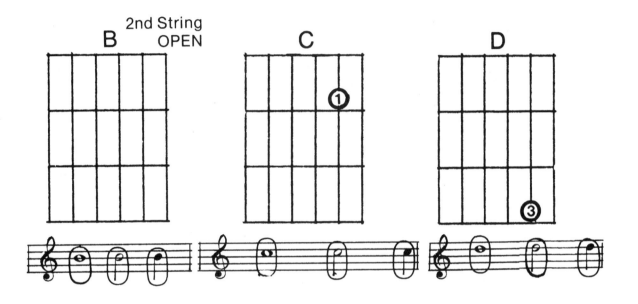

3RD STRING

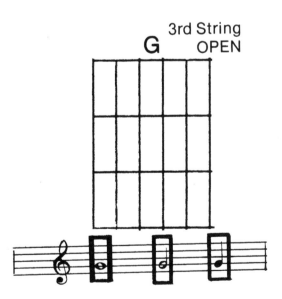

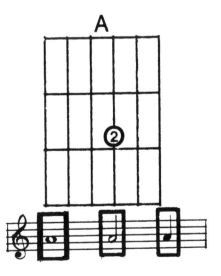

ON, TOP OF OLD SMOKY

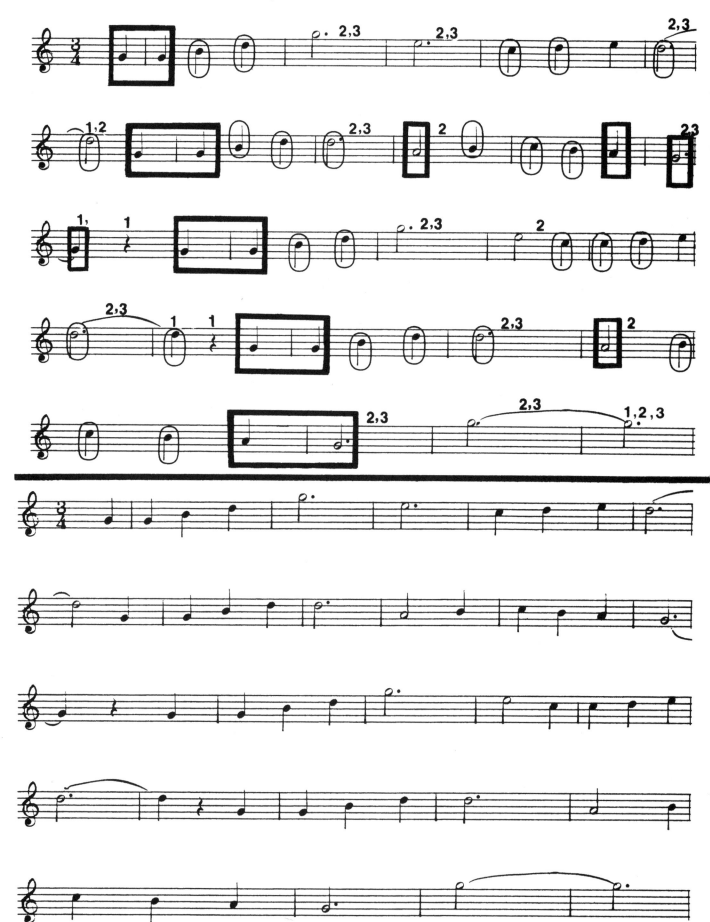

53

WHEN THE SAINTS GO MARCHING IN

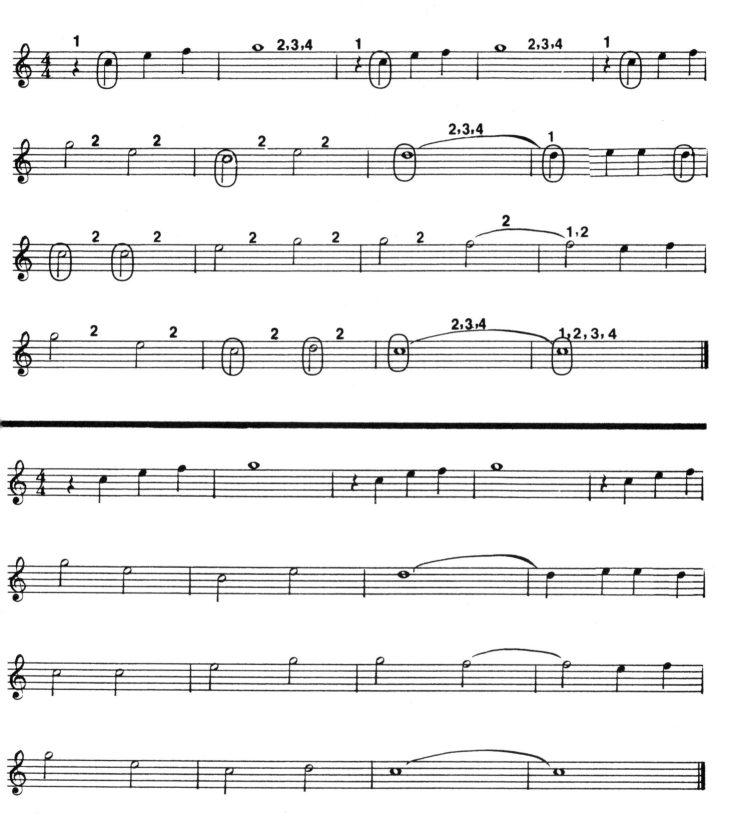

JINGLE BELLS

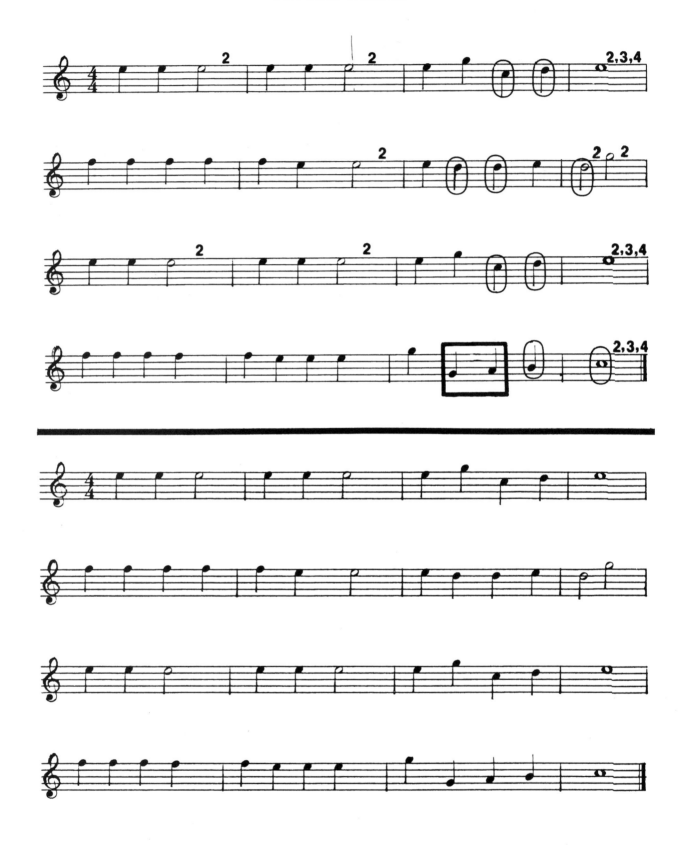

RED RIVER VALLEY

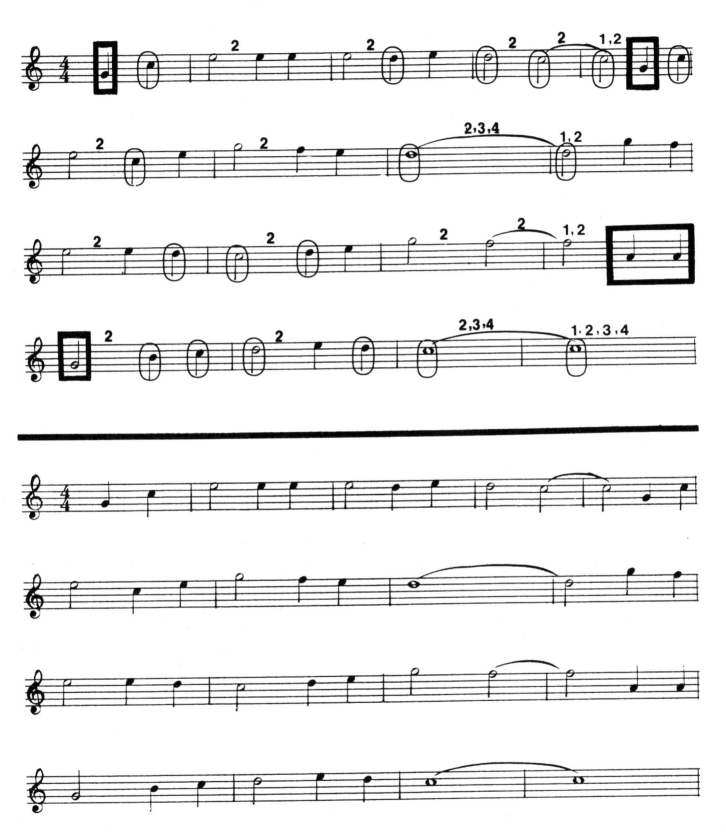

56

AURA LEE

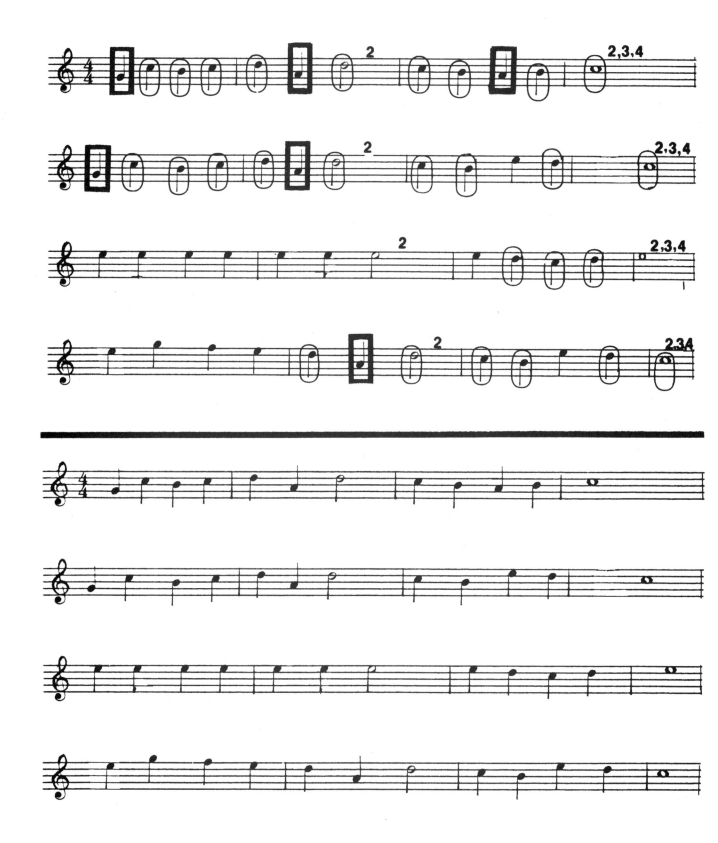

DAISY, DAISY
(On a Bicycle Built for Two)

EAST SIDE, WEST SIDE

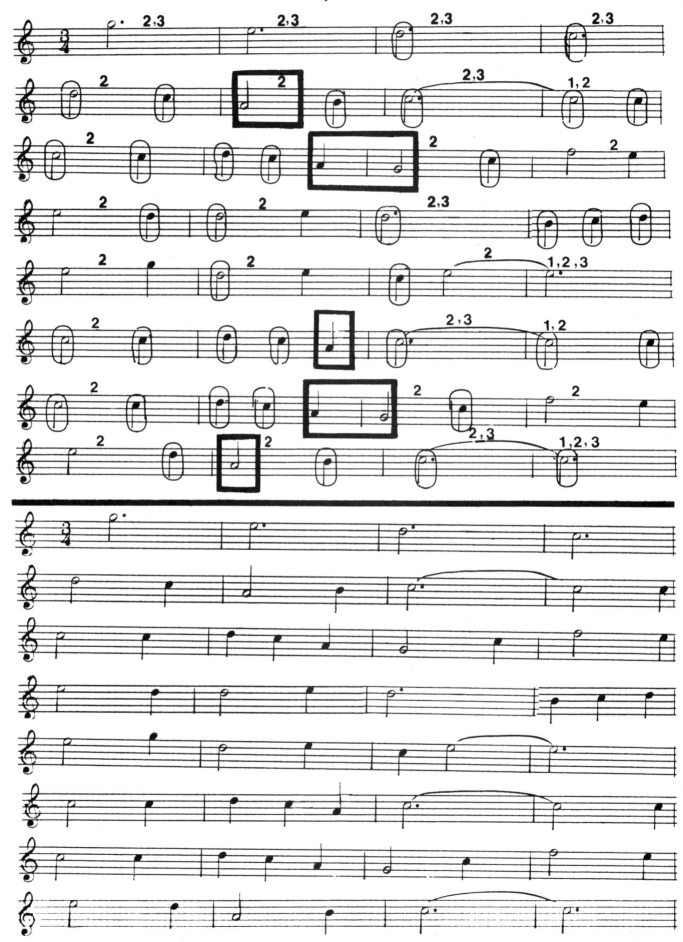

GOOD NIGHT LADIES

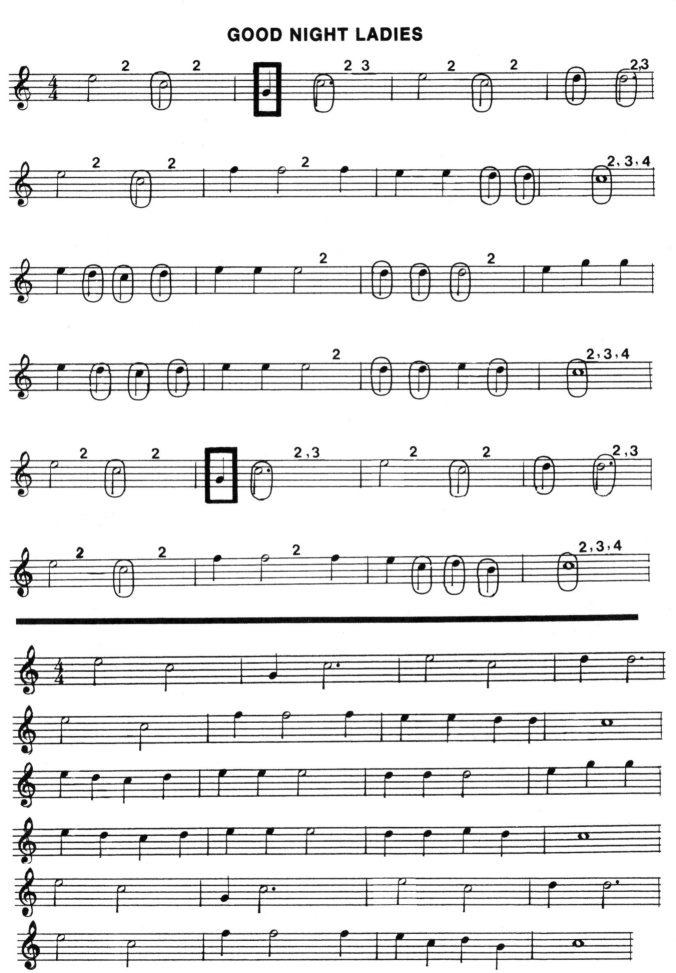

MORE CHORDS

We will be learning 3 chords in this lesson. The chords are A minor (AM) D seventh (D^7) and E seventh (E^7).

We will be using 3 fingers for Am and D^7, and 2 fingers for E^7.

THE A MINOR (AM) CHORD

1) To play **Am** you must place your **1st finger** on the **1st fret** of the **2nd string.** Put your **2nd finger** on the **2nd fret** of the **4th string.** Put your **3rd finger** on the **2nd fret** of the **3rd string.**

Am

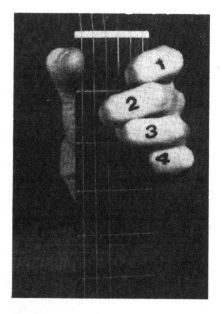

Am

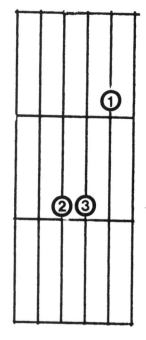

COMBINATION Am, G⁷, C

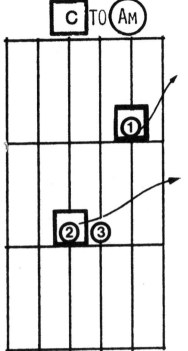

This position is the same for the Am and C chord.

This position is the same for the Am and the C chord.

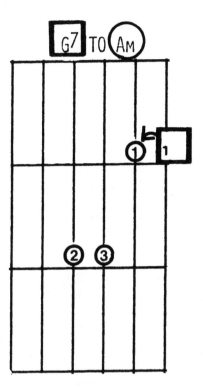

As you can see, your 1st and 2nd fingers are on the same frets for C and Am. Add your 3rd finger on the 2nd fret of the 3rd string and C becomes Am.

These flow charts try to emphasize that you move your fingers as little as possible. The less motion, the smoother and quicker the chord change.

The chord positions can be identified by rectangles and circles. If a rectangle and circle are on the same position on the guitar diagram it would mean that the finger position is the same for both chords.

EXERCISE

C   Am   G⁷   Am   C   G⁷   Am
///// ///// ///// ///// ///// ///// /////

THE D SEVENTH (D⁷) CHORD

1) To play **D⁷** you put your **1st finger** on the **1st fret** of the **2nd string**. You put your **2nd finger** on the **2nd fret** of the **3rd string**. You put your **3rd finger** on the **2nd fret** of the **1st string**.

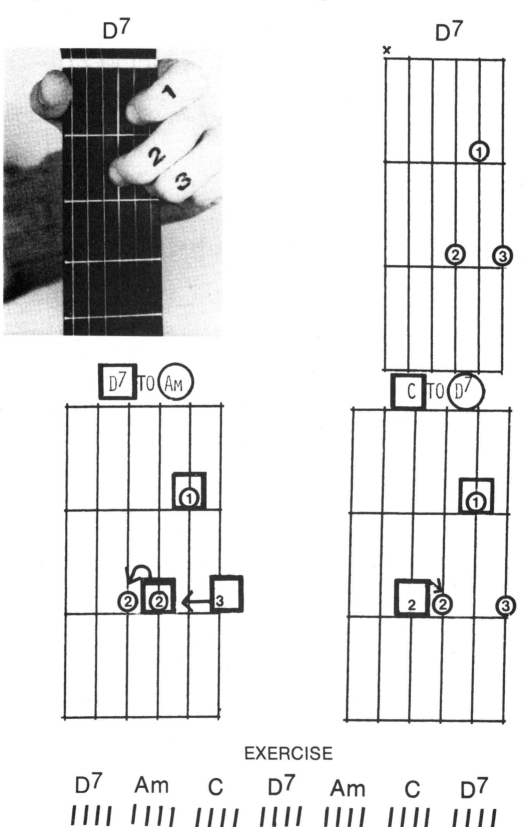

EXERCISE

D⁷	Am	C	D⁷	Am	C	D⁷
││││	││││	││││	││││	││││	││││	││││

THE E SEVENTH (E⁷) CHORD

1) The E^7 is the exact same finger position as C except it is up one string.

2) The same principles apply for E^7 as for C. Try to place both fingers down at the same time. Practice until you can play E^7 without looking at your fingers.

3) To play **E⁷** place your **1st finger** on the **1st fret** of the **3rd string**. Place your **2nd finger** on the **2nd fret** of the **5th string**.

E^7

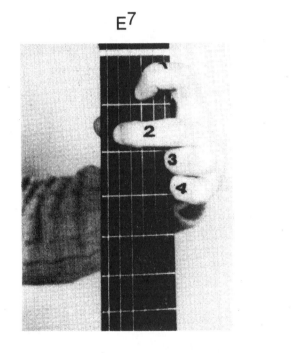

E^7

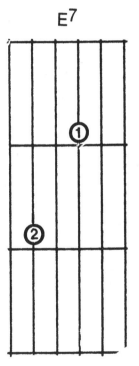

STUDENT'S NOTES

CHANGING FROM C TO E⁷ AND FROM G⁷ TO E⁷

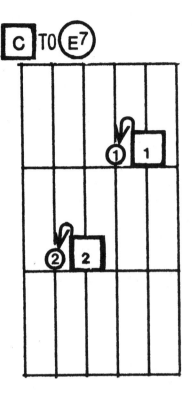

FLOW CHART C TO E⁷

As you can see on this Flow Chart, to change from C to E⁷ you move your 1st finger from the 1st fret of the 2nd string to the 1st fret of the 3rd string. At the same time move your 2nd finger from the 2nd fret of the 4th string to the 2nd fret of the 5th string. For E⁷ strike all the strings.

For changing from E⁷ to C reverse the process.

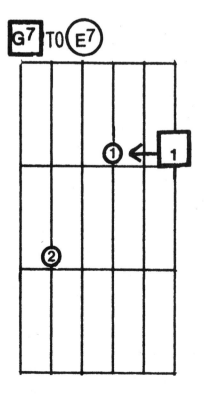

FLOW CHART G⁷ to E⁷

To change from G⁷ to E⁷ you must move your 1st finger from the 1st fret of the 1st string to the 1st fret of the 3rd string. At the same time put your 2nd finger on the 2nd fret of the 5th string.

HOME ON THE RANGE

G→   C→   G→
Oh give me a home, where the buf-fa-lo roam, Where the deer and the an-

D⁷→   G→   C→
te-lope play,   Where sel-dom is heard a dis-cour-ag-ing word, And

G→   D⁷→   G→   G→ C→   G→
the skies are not clou-dy all day.   Home, home on the range,

Aᴹ→   D⁷→   G→
Where the deer and the an-te-lope play,   Where sel-dom is heard a

C→   G→   D⁷→   G→
dis-cour-ag-ing word, and the skies are not cloud-y all day.

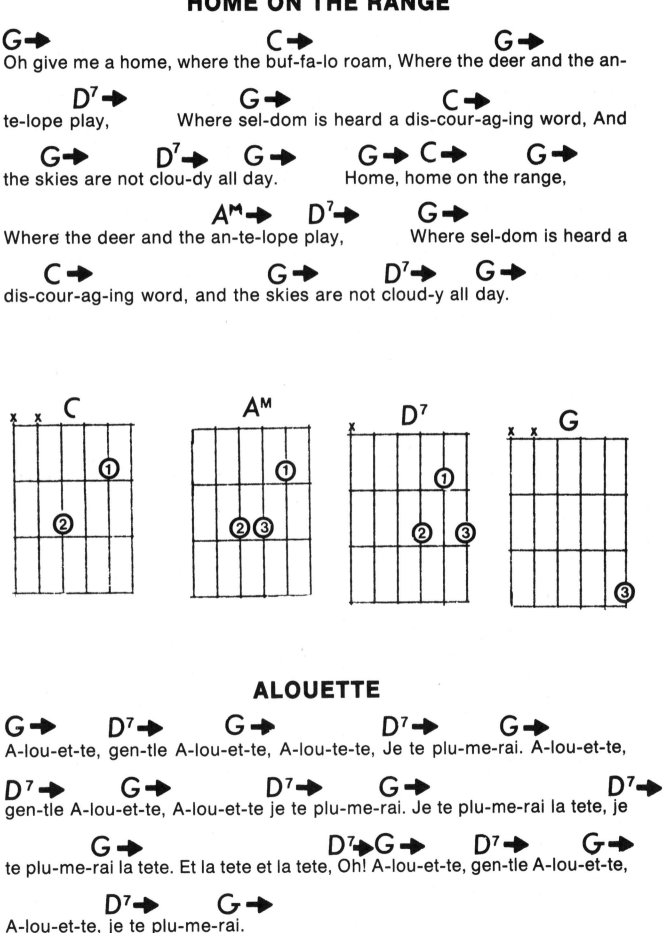

ALOUETTE

G→   D⁷→   G→   D⁷→   G→
A-lou-et-te, gen-tle A-lou-et-te, A-lou-te-te, Je te plu-me-rai. A-lou-et-te,

D⁷→   G→   D⁷→   G→   D⁷→
gen-tle A-lou-et-te, A-lou-et-te je te plu-me-rai. Je te plu-me-rai la tete, je

G→   D⁷→G→   D⁷→   G→
te plu-me-rai la tete. Et la tete et la tete, Oh! A-lou-et-te, gen-tle A-lou-et-te,

D⁷→   G→
A-lou-et-te, je te plu-me-rai.

WHEN JOHNNY COMES MARCHING HOME

Aᴹ➡   C➡
When John-ny comes march-ing home a-gain, Hur-rah, hur-rah! We'll give

Aᴹ➡   C➡   Aᴹ➡
him a heart-y wel-come then, Hur-rah, hur-rah! The men will cheer, the

E⁷➡   Aᴹ➡   E⁷➡   AᴹE⁷Aᴹ E⁷
boys will shout, The la-dies, they will all turn out, And we'll all feel gay, When

Aᴹ➡   E⁷➡   Aᴹ➡
John-ny comes march-ing home.

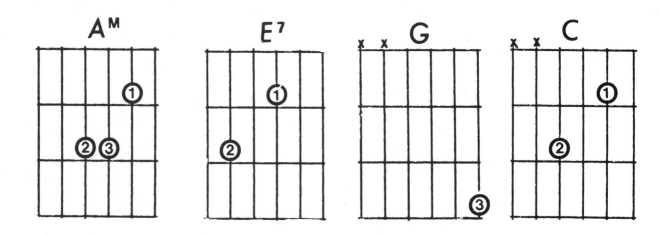

MICHAEL, ROW THE BOAT ASHORE

G➡   G➡G➡
Mich-ael, row the boat a-shore, Hal-le-lu-jah! Mich-ael, row the boat a-

Aᴹ➡   G➡C G
shore, Hal-le-lu-jah!

WHAT CHILD IS THIS? (Green-Sleeves)

A^M ▶   G →   A^M →
What child is this,   who laid to rest,   on Ma-ry's lap   is

E⁷ →   A^M →   G →
sleep-ing? Whom an-gels greet   with an-thems sweet   while

A^M →   E⁷ →   A^M →   C →   G →
shep-herds watch   are keep-ing? This, this   is Christ the

           A^M →   E⁷ →
King;   Who shep-herds guard   and an-gels sing; Haste,

C →   G →   A^M →   E⁷ →
haste,   to bring Him laud,   the Babe   the Son   of

A^M →
Ma-ry.

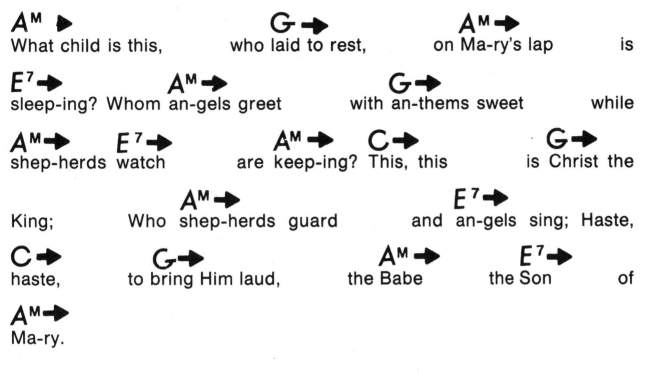

ON TOP OF OLD SMOKY

C →   G →   D⁷ →
On top of old smoky, All covered with snow, I lost my true lover A-cortin' too

G → C →   G →   D⁷ →
slow. A-courtin's a pleasure, A-flertin's a grief, A false-hearted lover Is

       G →
worse than a thief.

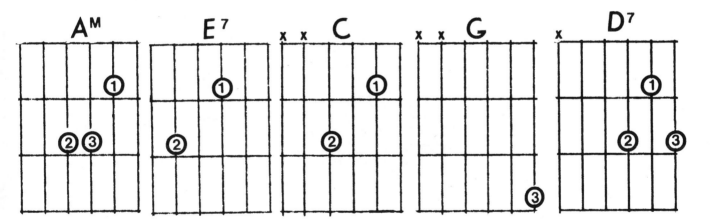

THE NOTES ON THE 4TH STRING

1) The names of the notes on the 4th string are D, E, and F. These notes have the same names as three notes you have already learned on previous strings. These notes will be practiced with the previous D, E, and F you have learned for review and also to avoid confusion.

2) TO PLAY  Any note placed on this position of the musical staff is D.

D = Strike the 4th string without putting down any fingers of your left hand.

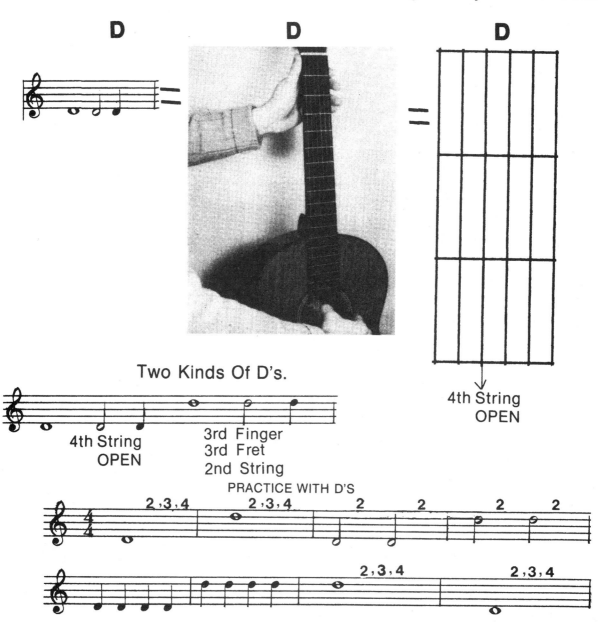

D **D** **D**

Two Kinds Of D's.

4th String OPEN

3rd Finger
3rd Fret
2nd String

4th String OPEN

PRACTICE WITH D'S

2,3,4   2,3,4   2   2   2   2

2,3,4   2,3,4

THE EIGHTH NOTES

1) These D's are in the form of eighth notes.

2) An eighth note, when it is by itself, will look like ♪ or ♪ . When two or more eighth notes are put together they will be connected with a straight line ♫ ♫ . These are not to be confused with ties. Ties are connected by looped lines. Also unlike notes that are tied, each eighth note is played.

3) An eighth note is worth half a beat. Two eighth notes would equal one quarter note in time. How do you count half a beat? Whenever you see an eighth note, speed it up. How much do you speed it up? This is something you must feel. **You should play an eighth note twice as fast as a quarter note.**

EIGHTH NOTES USING D (4TH STRING)

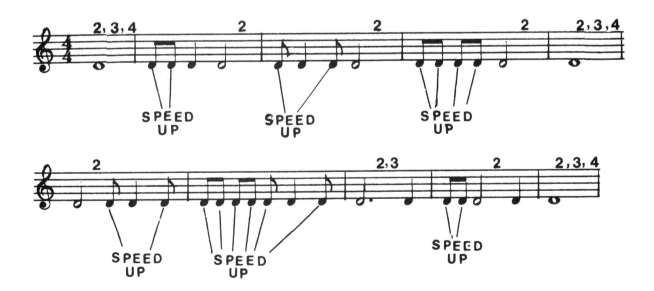

LEARNING E ON THE 4TH STRING

1) The next note we are going to learn on the 4th string is E.

2) To play **E** you put your **2nd finger** on the **2nd fret** of the **4th string.**

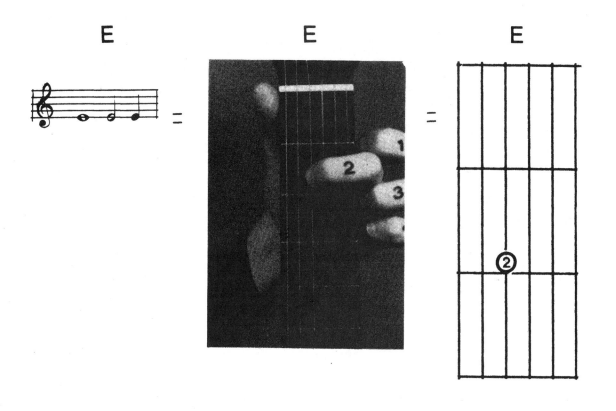

E　　　　　　　　E　　　　　　　　E

Two Kinds Of E's

2nd Finger	1st String
2nd Fret	OPEN
4th String	

Practice With E's

LEARNING F ON THE 4TH STRING

1) The next note we are going to learn on the 4th string is F.

2) To play **F** you put your **3rd finger** on the **3rd fret** of the **4th string.**

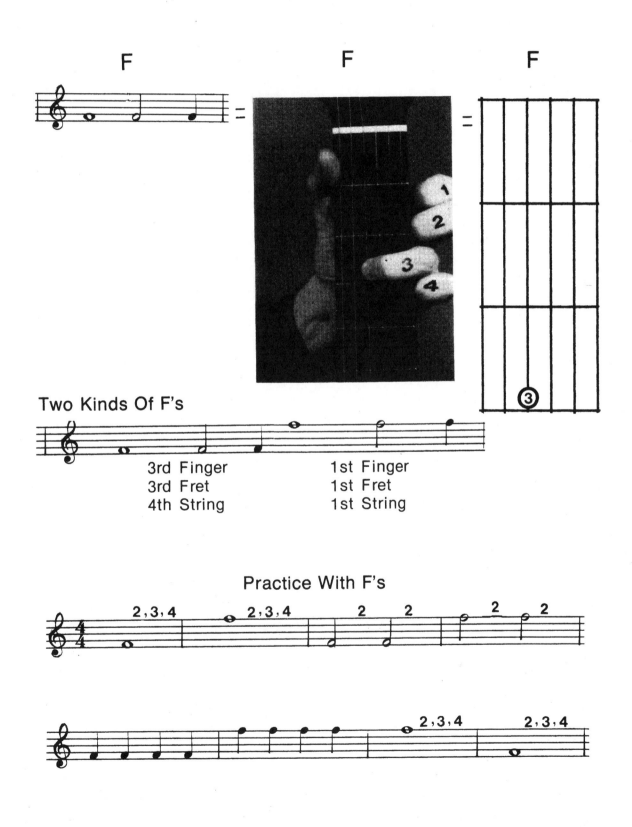

Two Kinds Of F's

3rd Finger	1st Finger
3rd Fret	1st Fret
4th String	1st String

Practice With F's

THE DOTTED QUARTER NOTE ♩♪·

1)

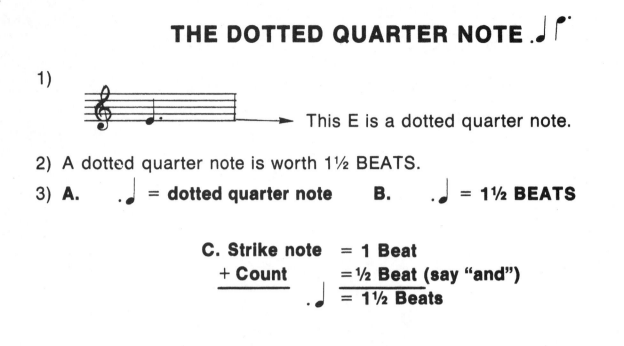

This E is a dotted quarter note.

2) A dotted quarter note is worth 1½ BEATS.

3) **A.**   ♩· = **dotted quarter note**   **B.**   ♩· = **1½ BEATS**

C. Strike note   = 1 Beat
+ Count   = ½ Beat (say "and")

♩· = **1½ Beats**

4) How do you count half a beat? We learned with eighth notes to count half a beat. However, you say "and" after you play the note. In other words, there is a slight pause or hesitation before you play the next note. A dotted quarter note is usually preceded or followed by an eighth note.

EXERCISE

SYMBOL CODED NOTE CHART

3RD STRING

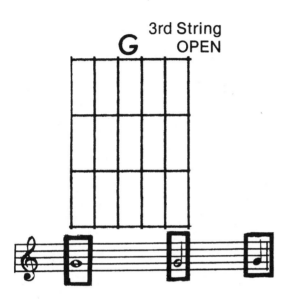

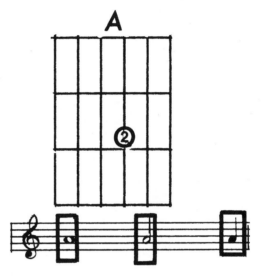

4TH STRING

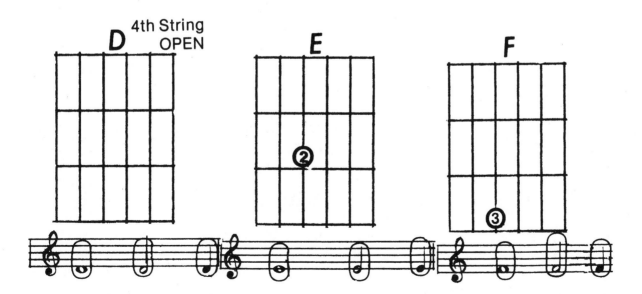

THIS OLD MAN

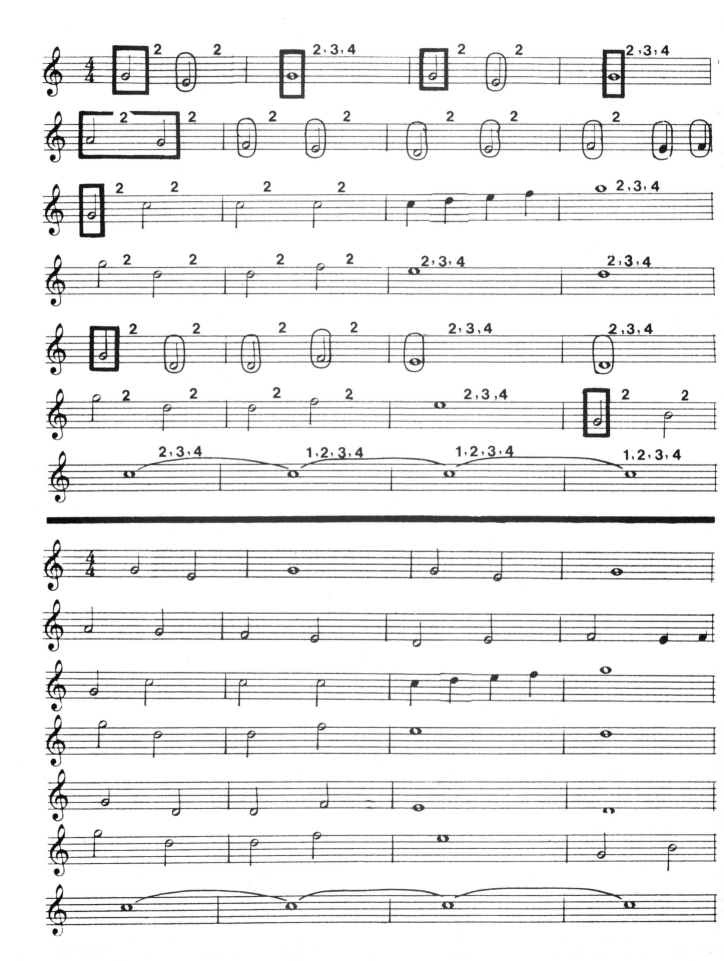

SILENT NIGHT

+ **Indicates that you say "and" after the note. In other words there is a slight pause after the note.**

O **Indicates that you speed the note up.**

WHEN JOHNNY COMES MARCHING HOME

MY BONNIE

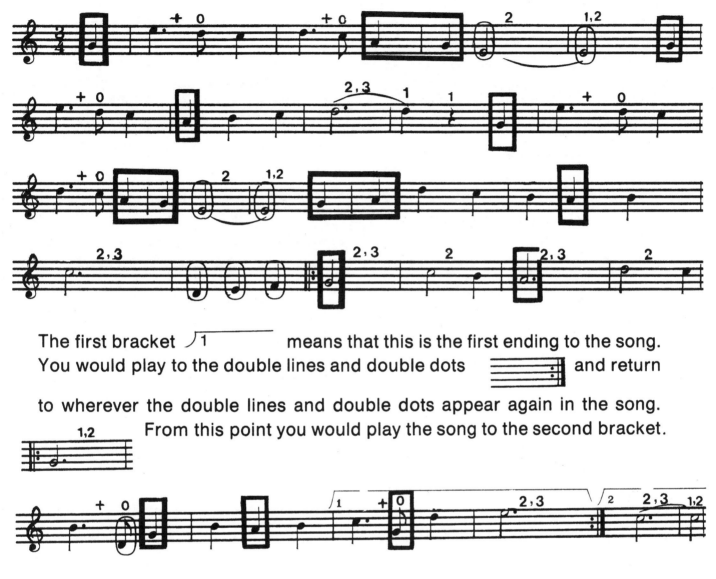

The first bracket ⌐1 means that this is the first ending to the song. You would play to the double lines and double dots and return

to wherever the double lines and double dots appear again in the song. From this point you would play the song to the second bracket.

The second time through you would skip the first bracket

and proceed directly to second bracket.

78

TOM DOOLEY

AULD LANG SYNE

BACK TO CHORDS

We are going to learn 3 new chords. They are D, A seventh (A^7) and A

THE D CHORD

1) To play D you put your **1st finger** on the **2nd fret** of the **3rd string.** You put your **2nd finger** on the **2nd fret** of the **1st string.** You put your **3rd finger** on the **3rd fret** of the **2nd string.**

D

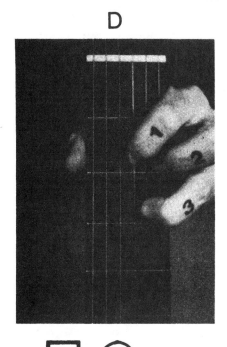

D

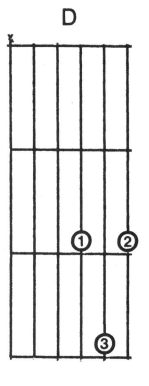

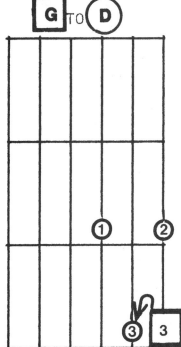

EXERCISE

G	D	G	D	G
/ / / /	/ / / /	/ / / /	/ / / /	/ / / /

D	G	D	G	D
/ / / /	/ / / /	/ / / /	/ / / /	/ / / /

THE A SEVENTH (A⁷) CHORD

1) To play **A⁷** you put your **1st finger** on the **2nd fret** of the **4th string.** You put your **2nd finger** on the **2nd fret** of the **2nd string.**

A7

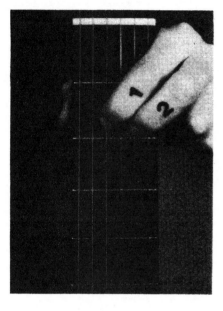

A⁷

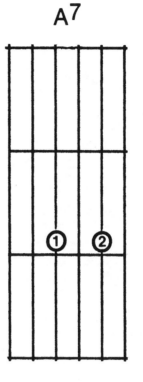

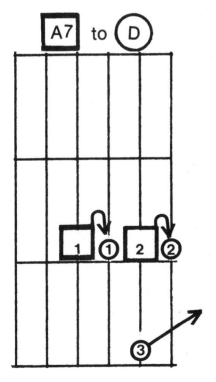

EXERCISE

A⁷	D	A⁷	D	A⁷
IIII	IIII	IIII	IIII	IIII

D	A⁷	D	A⁷	D
IIII	IIII	IIII	IIII	IIII

Add your third finger to form D.

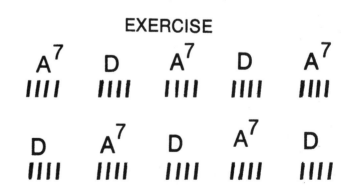

THE A CHORD

1) To play **A** you put your **1st finger** on the **2nd fret** of the **4th string.** You put your **2nd finger** on the **2nd fret** of the **3rd string.** You put your **3rd finger** on the **2nd fret** of the **2nd string.**

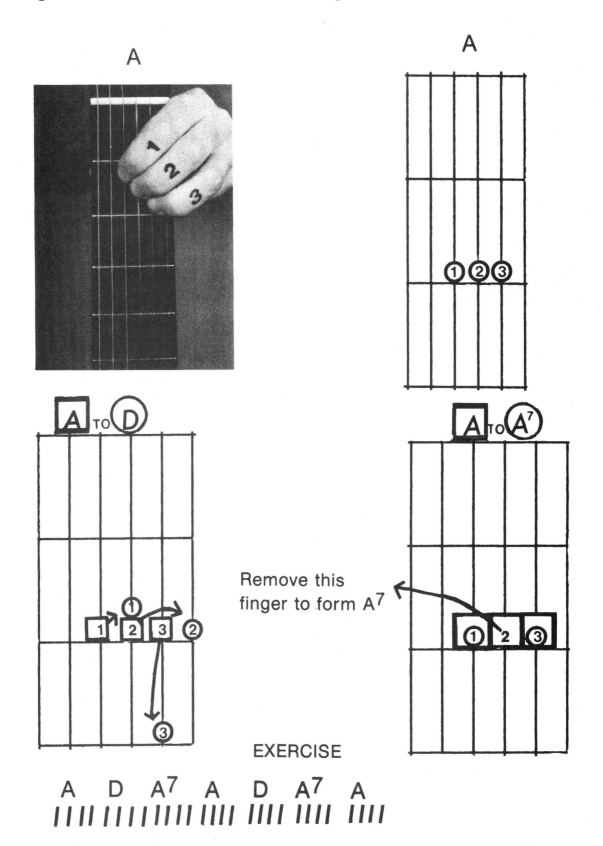

Remove this finger to form A⁷

EXERCISE

A   D   A⁷   A   D   A⁷   A

HERE WE GO ROUND THE MULBERRY-BUSH

D ➡   A⁷ ➡
Here we go round the mul-ber-ry bush, the mul-ber-ry bush, the mul-ber-

        D ➡   A⁷➡   D ➡
ry bush, Here we go round the mul-ber-ry bush, So ear-ly in the morn-ing.

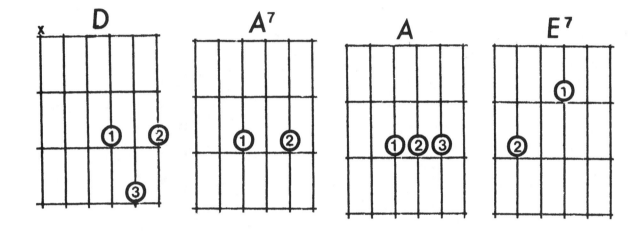

JINGLE BELLS

A ➡   D➡   A➡
Jin-gle bells, jin-gle bells, jin-gle all the way! Oh, what fun it is to ride in a

E⁷ ➡   A ➡   D➡
one-horse o-pen sleigh! Jin-gle bells, jin-gle bells, jin-gle all the way! Oh,

        A➡   E⁷➡   A➡
what fun it is to ride in a one-horse o-pen sleigh!

BLOW THE MAN DOWN

A➡   **E**⁷➡

Blow the man down bul-lies, blow the man down, to me way, Hey! Blow the

man down, blow the man down bul-lies, blow him away, give me some time

A➡

to blow the man down.

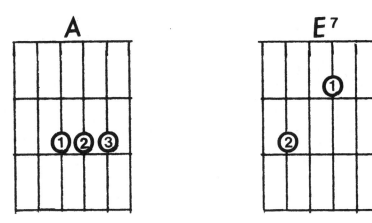

THE FARMER IN THE DELL

A➡

Oh, the farm-er in the dell,   the farm-er in the dell,   Hi-ho the

              E⁷➡   **A**➡

der-ry-o, the farm-er in the dell.

COMIN' ROUND THE MOUNTAIN

D ➡
She'll be com-in' round the moun-tain when she comes, she'll be com-in'

          A⁷ ➡   **D** ➡   **D⁷** ➡
round the moun-tain when she comes, she'll be com-in' round the moun-

    G ➡   **A⁷** ➡
tain, she'll be com-in' round the moun-tain, she'll be com-in' round the

    D ➡
moun-tain when she comes.

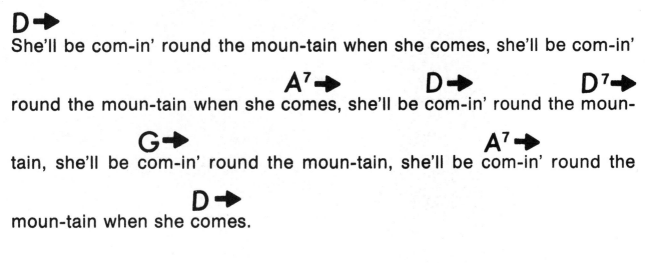

HE'S GOT THE WHOLE WORLD IN HIS HANDS

          D ➡   **A⁷** ➡
He's got the whole world in His hands, He's got the whole world in His

          D ➡   **A⁷** ➡
hands, He's got the whole world in His hands, He's got the whole world in

D ➡
His hands

CAMPTOWN RACES

A➡   E⁷➡   A➡

De camptown ladies sing dis song, Doo-dah! doo-dah! De camptown race

　　　　　　　　E⁷➡   A➡   D➡

track five miles long, Oh! doo-dah day! Goin' to run all night! Goin' to run all

A➡   E⁷➡   A➡

day! I'll bet my money on de bobtail nag, Somebody bet on de bay!

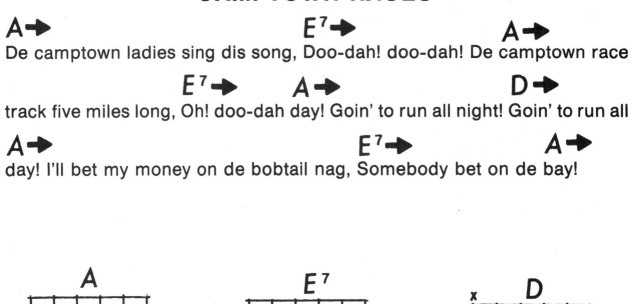

GIVE ME THAT OLD TIME RELIGION

A➡   E⁷➡   A➡

Give me that old time re-lig-ion, Give me that old time re-lig-ion, Give me

　　　　　　D➡   A➡ E⁷➡   A➡

that old time re-lig-ion, It's good e-nough for me. It was good for the He-

　　　　　E⁷➡   A➡

brew chil-dren, It was good for the He-brew chil-dren, It was good for the

　　　　D➡   A➡ E⁷➡   A➡

He-brew chil-dren, And it's good e-nough for me. Give me that

OH, SUSANNA

A➡
I've come from Al-a-ba-ma With my ban-jo on my knee. I'm going to Loui-
                                            E⁷➡   **A**➡

D➡ **A**➡
si-an-a, My Susanna for to see; It rained all day the night I left, The weath-

E⁷➡ **A**➡   **D**➡   **A**➡**D**➡
er it was dry; The sun so hot I froze myself; Su-san-na, don't you cry. Oh,

       A➡   **E**⁷➡**A**➡
Su-   san-na, Oh, don't you cry for me, I come from Al-a-ba-ma With

D➡ **A**➡
my ban-jo on my knee.

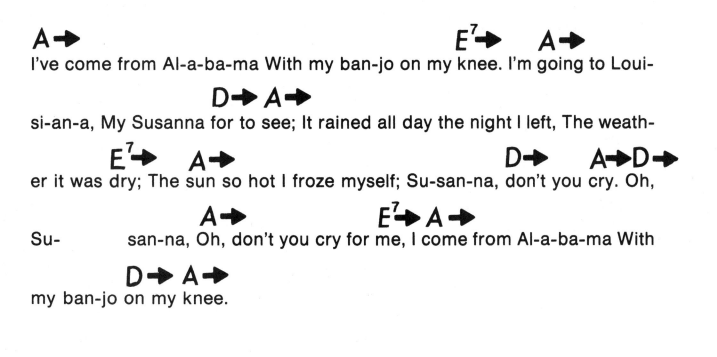

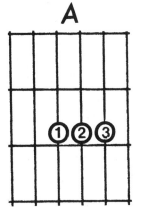
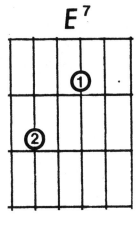
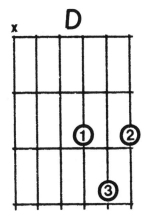

TOM DOOLEY

A➡   **E**⁷➡
Met her on the hill-top, there I took her life, Met her on the hill-top, stabbed

      A➡
her with my knife. Hang down your head, Tom Doo-ley, Hand down your

E⁷➡   **A**➡
head and cry, killed poor Laura Foster, you know you're bound to die.

88

THE NOTES ON THE 5TH STRING

1) The names of the notes on the 5th string are A, B, and C. These notes have the same names as three notes you have already learned.

2) To play A

A   A   A

Two Kinds Of A's

5th string
open

2nd finger
2nd fret
3rd string

5th string
open

PRACTICE WITH A's

THE B NOTE ON THE 5TH STRING

TO PLAY B

B = B = B

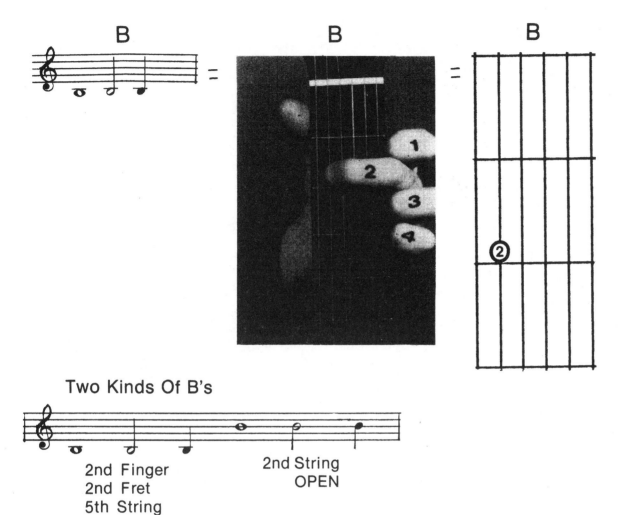

Two Kinds Of B's

2nd Finger
2nd Fret
5th String

2nd String
OPEN

PRACTICE WITH B's

Notes on the 5th and 6th string must
be held down firmly or they will rattle.

THE C NOTE ON THE 5TH STRING

TO PLAY C

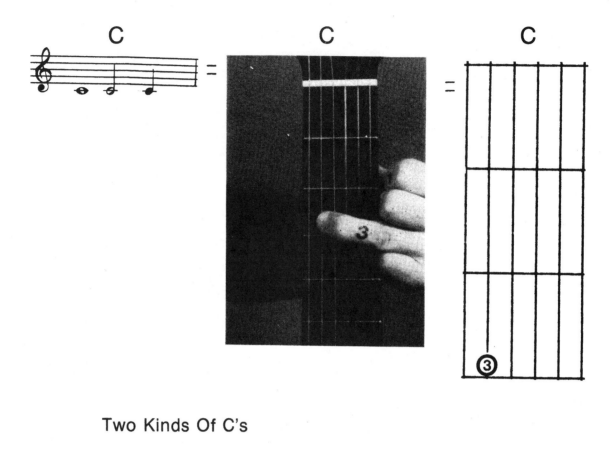

Two Kinds Of C's

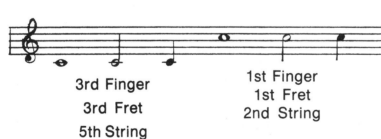

3rd Finger
3rd Fret
5th String

1st Finger
1st Fret
2nd String

PRACTICE WITH C's

SYMBOL CODED NOTE CHART

4TH STRING

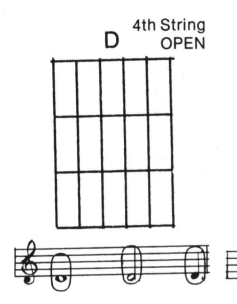
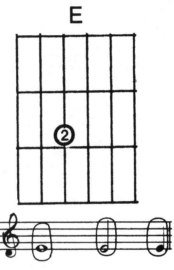
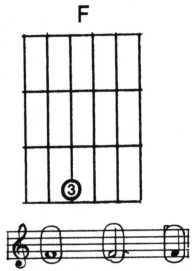

5TH STRING

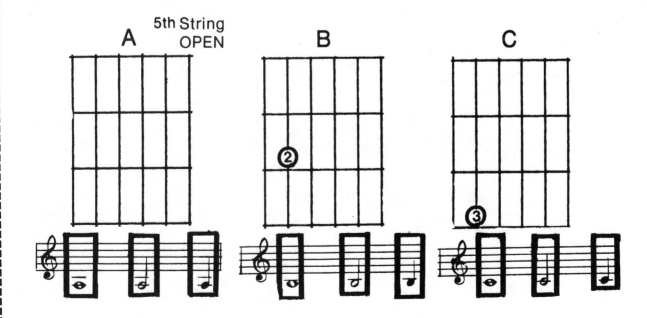

92

OH SUSANNA

BLOW THE MAN DOWN

MICHAEL, ROW THE BOAT ASHORE

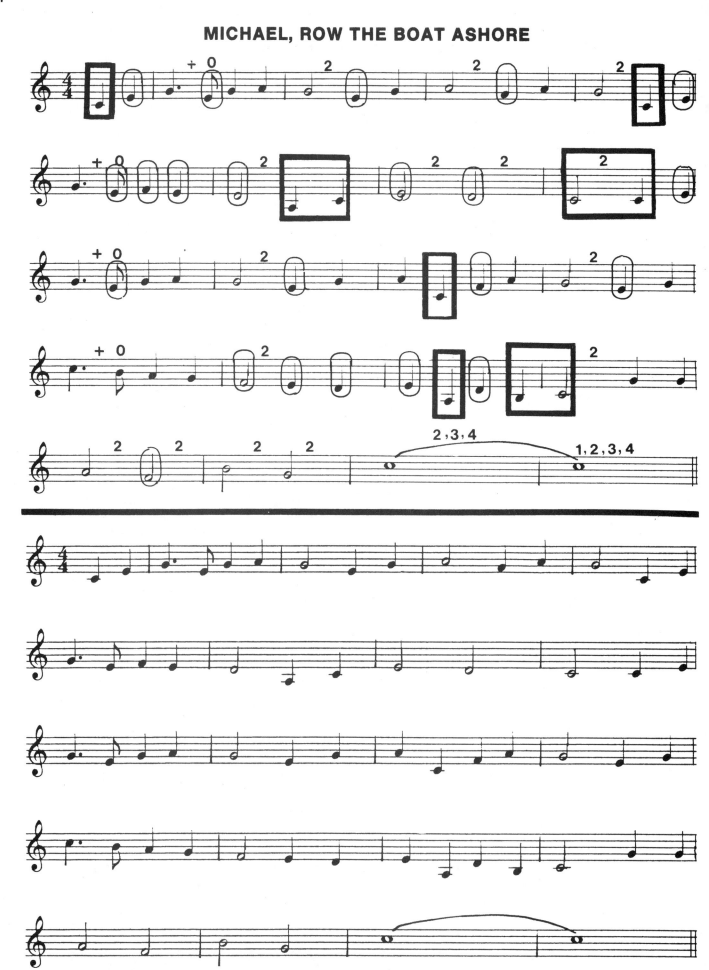

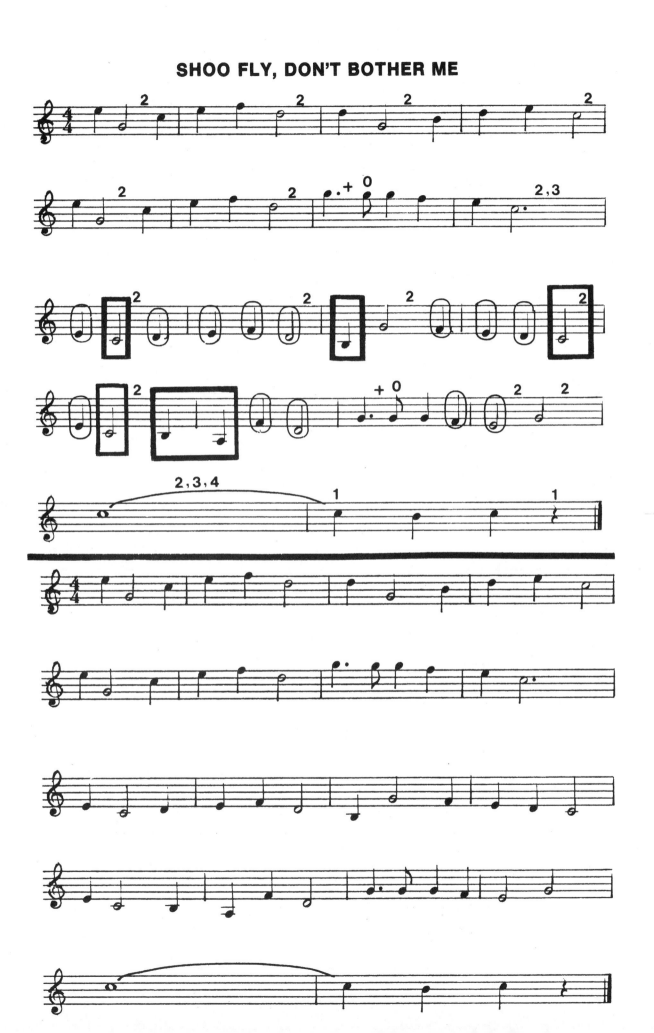

SHOO FLY, DON'T BOTHER ME

THE YELLOW ROSE OF TEXAS

JOSHUA FIT THE BATTLE OF JERICHO

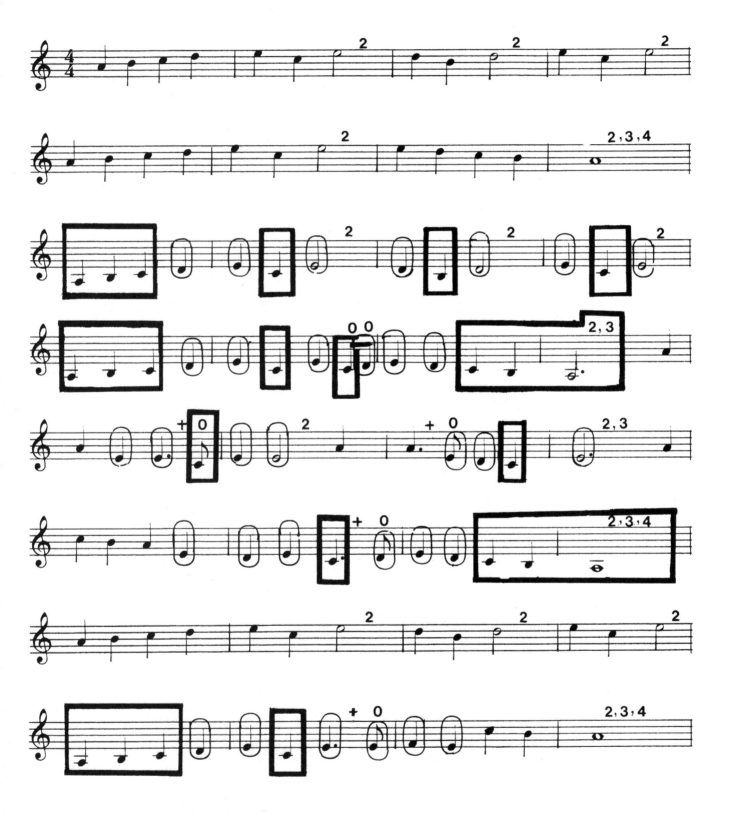

JOSHUA FIT THE BATTLE OF JERICHO

THREE MORE CHORDS

1) We are going to learn two new chords:E, D minor (Dm) and a fuller form of a chord we already learned: C.

2) To play **E** you put your **1st finger** on the **1st fret** of the **3rd string.** You put your **2nd finger** on the **2nd fret** of the **5th string.** You put your **3rd finger** on the **2nd fret** of the **4th string.**

E

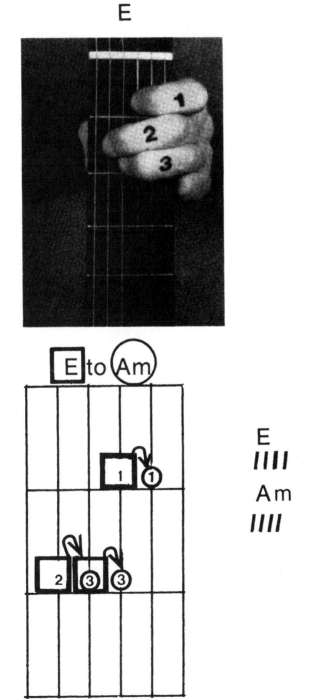

E

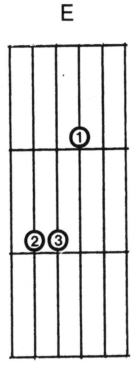

EXERCISE

E	Am	E	Am	E
////	////	////	////	////
Am	E	Am	E	A
////	//// ////		////	////

THE D MINOR (Dm) CHORD

To play **Dm** you put your **1st finger** on the **1st fret** of the **1st string**. Put your **2nd finger**, on the **2nd fret** of the **3rd string**. Put your **3rd finger** on the **3rd fret** of the **2nd string**.

Dm

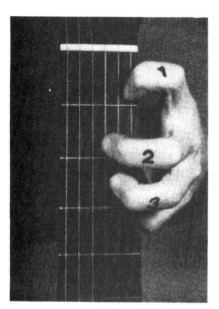

Dm

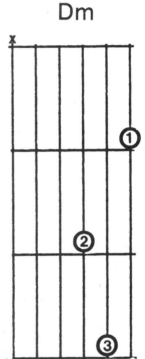

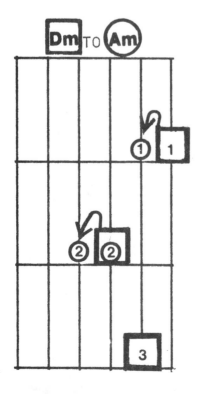

EXERCISE

Dm	Am	Dm	Am	Dm
////	////	////	////	////

Am	Dm	Dm	Am	Am
////	////	////	////	////

THE C CHORD

1) There are many different forms of the same chord as there are many different forms of the same note. This C CHORD is a fuller and more complete chord.

2) To play **C** you put your **1st finger** on the **1st fret** of the **2nd string**. You put your **2nd finger** on the **2nd fret** of the **4th string**. You put your **3rd finger** on the **3rd fret** of the **5th string**.

C

C

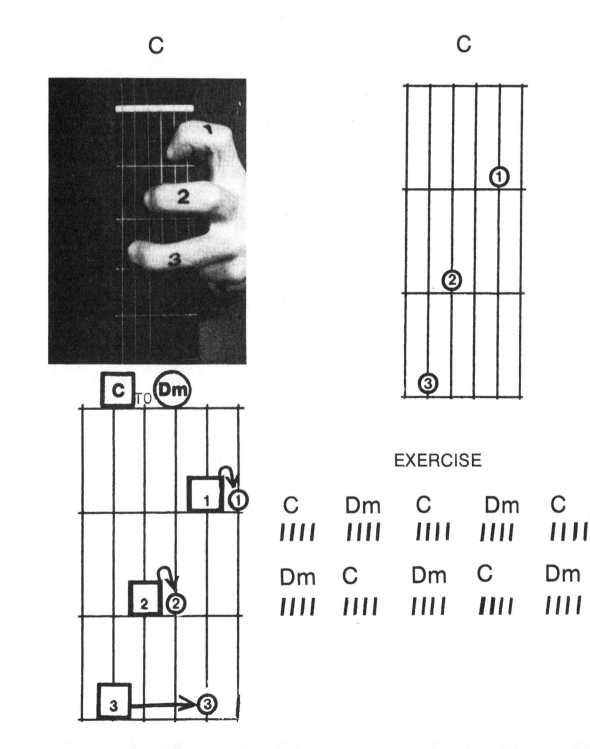

C To Dm

EXERCISE

C	Dm	C	Dm	C
////	////	////	////	////

Dm	C	Dm	C	Dm
////	////	////	////	////

BEAUTIFUL DREAMER

C →   **D**ᴹ →   **G**⁷ →
Beau-ti-ful dream-er wake un-to me.   Star-light and dew drops are

C →
wait-ing for thee;   Sounds of the rude world heard in the day,

G⁷ →   **C** →   **G**⁷ →
Lulled by the moon-light have all passed a-way!   Beau-ti-ful dream-

C →   **D**ᴹ →   **G**⁷ →
er, queen of my song,   list while I woo thee with soft mel-o-dy;

C →   **D**ᴹ →   **G**⁷ →
Gone are the cares of life's bus-y throng,   beau-ti-ful dream-er a-

C →
wake un-to me.

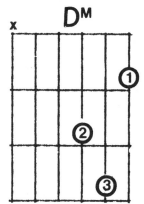

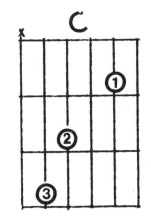

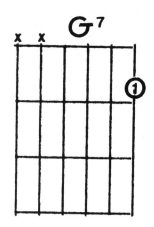

SCARBOROUGH FAIR

A^M→   G→   A^M→C→   A^M→   C→

Oh where are you go-ing to Scar-bor-ough fair, sa-vory, sage, rose-ma-ry,

E→   A^M→   C→   G→E→A^M→   G→

and thyme; Re-mem-ber me to a lass that lives there, For once she was a

A^M→

true love of mine.

AM   x x G   E   x C

A   x D

AULD LANG SYNE

A→   E→   A→

Should auld ac-quaint-ance be for-got, And nev-er brought to

D→   A→   E→   D→

mind?   Should auld ac-quaint-ance be for-got, And days of auld lang

A→   E→   A→   D→

syne?   For auld-lang-syne, my dear,   For auld-land-syne;

A→   E→   D→   A→

We'll take a cup o' kind-ness yet For auld-lang-syne.

JOSHUA FIT THE BATTLE OF JERICHO

Dᴹ➡
Josh-ua fit the bat-tle of Jer-i-cho,

A⁷➡
Jer-i-cho,

Dᴹ➡
Jer-i-

cho,

Dᴹ➡
Josh-ua fit the bat-tle of Jer-i-cho,

A⁷➡
And the walls came tumb-ling

Dᴹ➡
down, that morn-ing

Dᴹ➡
Josh-ua fit the bat-tle of Jer-i-cho,

A⁷➡
Jer-i-cho,

Dᴹ➡
Jer-i-cho,

Dᴹ➡
Josh-ua fit the bat-tle of Jer-i-cho,

A⁷➡
And the walls came tumb-ling

Dᴹ➡
down.

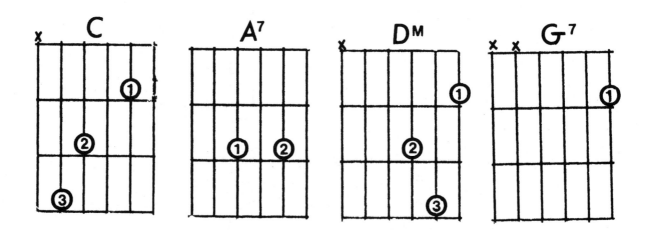

THE NOTES ON THE SIXTH STRING

The names of the 3 notes on the sixth string are E, F, and G. These notes have the same names as other notes you have learned.

TO PLAY E

Three Kinds Of E's

6th string
open

2nd finger
2nd fret
4th string

1st string open

PRACTICE WITH E's

THE F NOTE ON THE SIXTH STRING

TO PLAY F

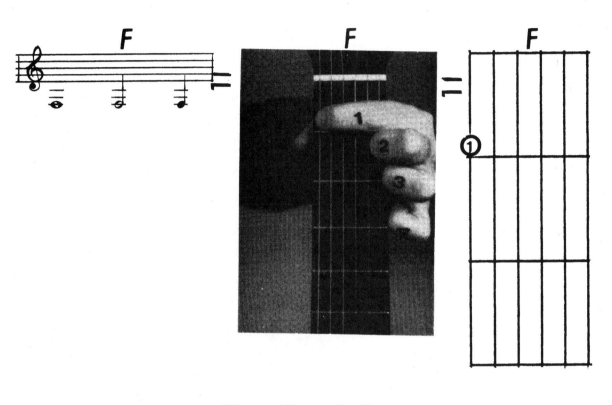

F   F   F

Three Kinds Of F's

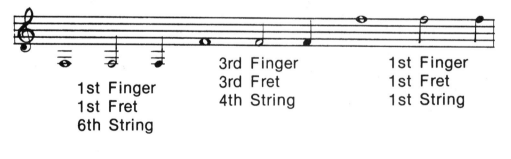

1st Finger
1st Fret
6th String

3rd Finger
3rd Fret
4th String

1st Finger
1st Fret
1st String

PRACTICE WITH F's

THE G NOTE ON THE SIXTH STRING

TO PLAY G

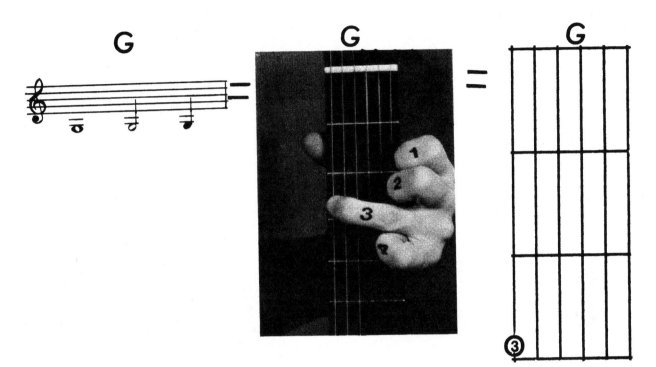

Three Kinds Of G's

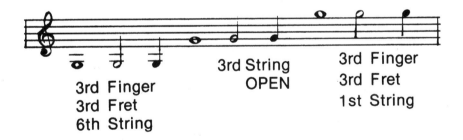

3rd Finger
3rd Fret
6th String

3rd String
OPEN

3rd Finger
3rd Fret
1st String

PRACTICE WITH G's

SYMBOL CODED NOTE CHART

5TH STRING

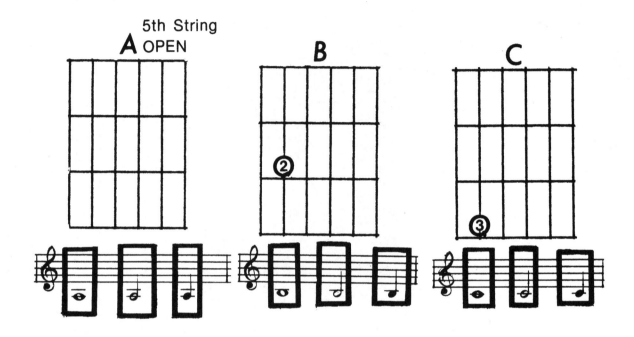

6TH STRING

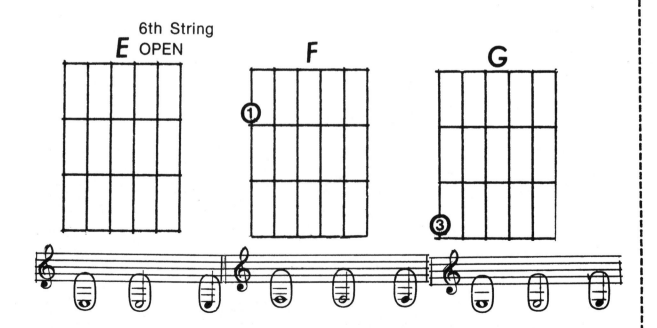

SCARBOROUGH FAIR

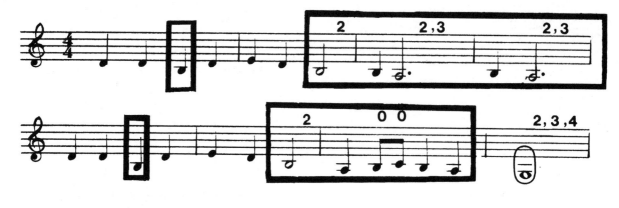

CAMPTOWN RACES

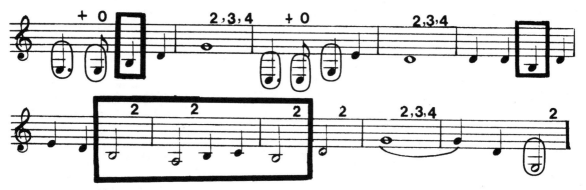

LONG LONG AGO

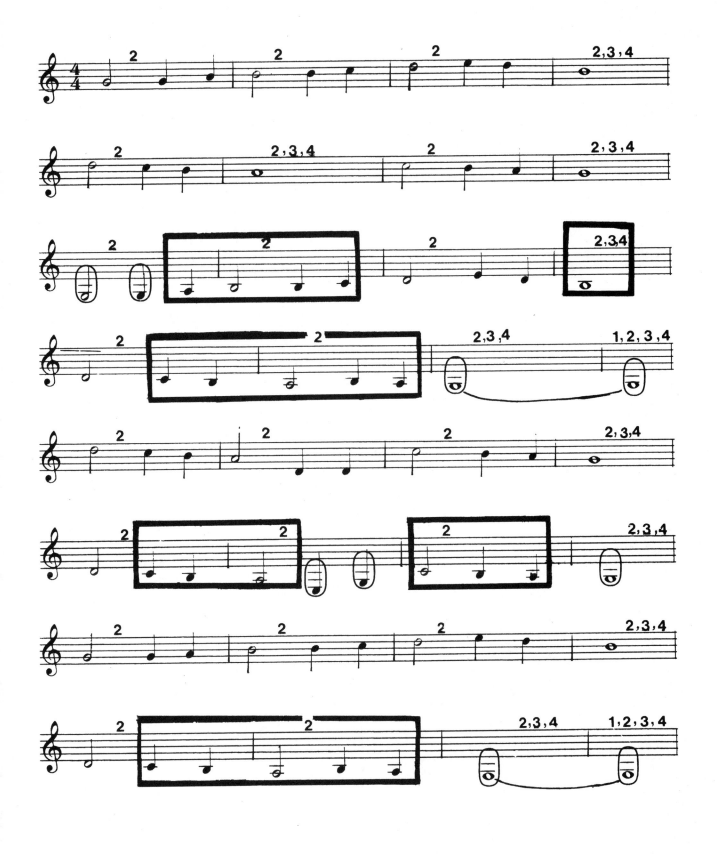

LONG LONG AGO

MY OLD KENTUCKY HOME

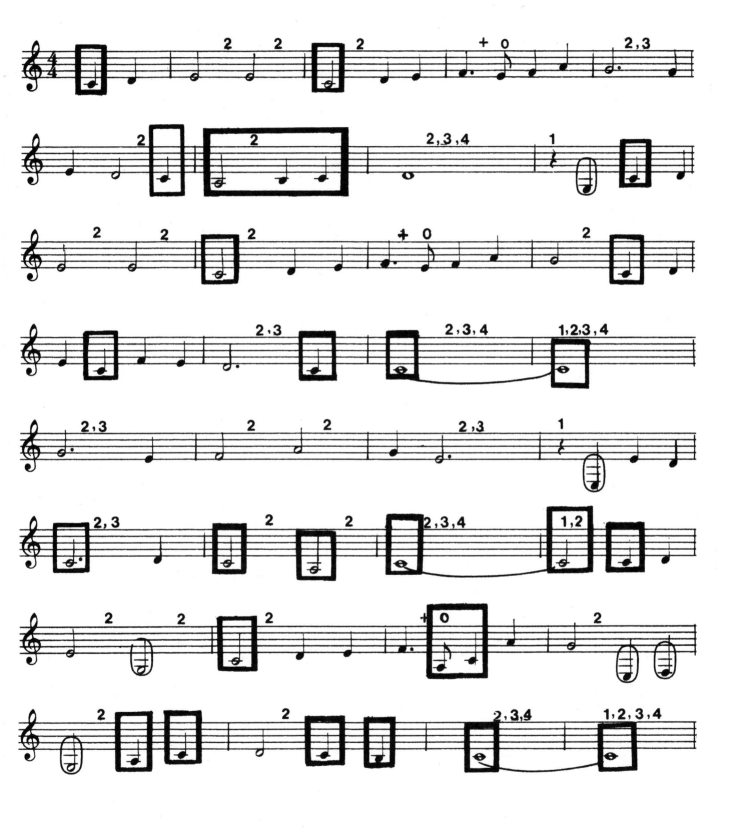

MY OLD KENTUCKY HOME

LONDONDERRY AIR

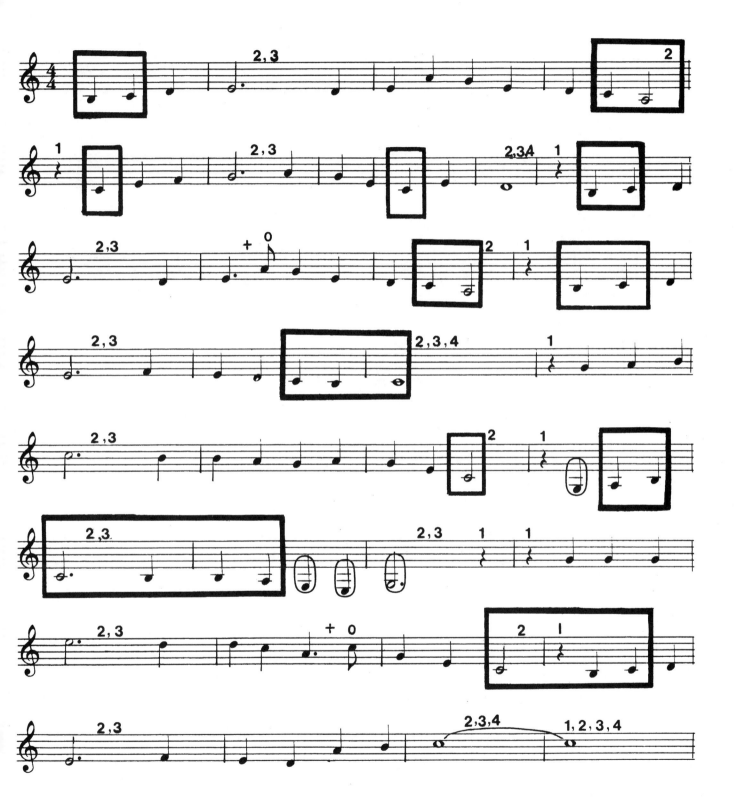

LONDONDERRY AIR

I'VE BEEN WORKING ON THE RAILROAD

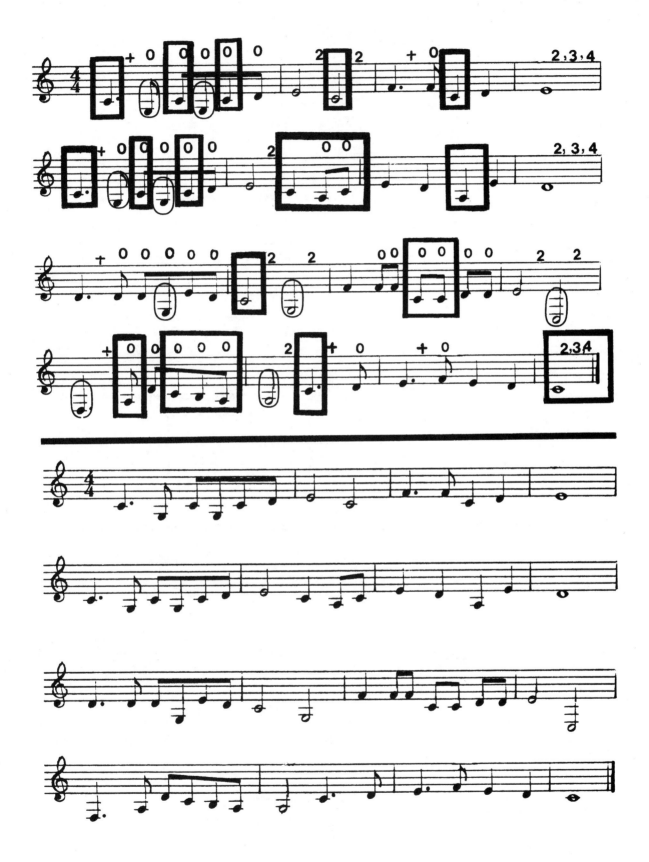

118

CARRY ME BACK TO OLD VIRGINNY

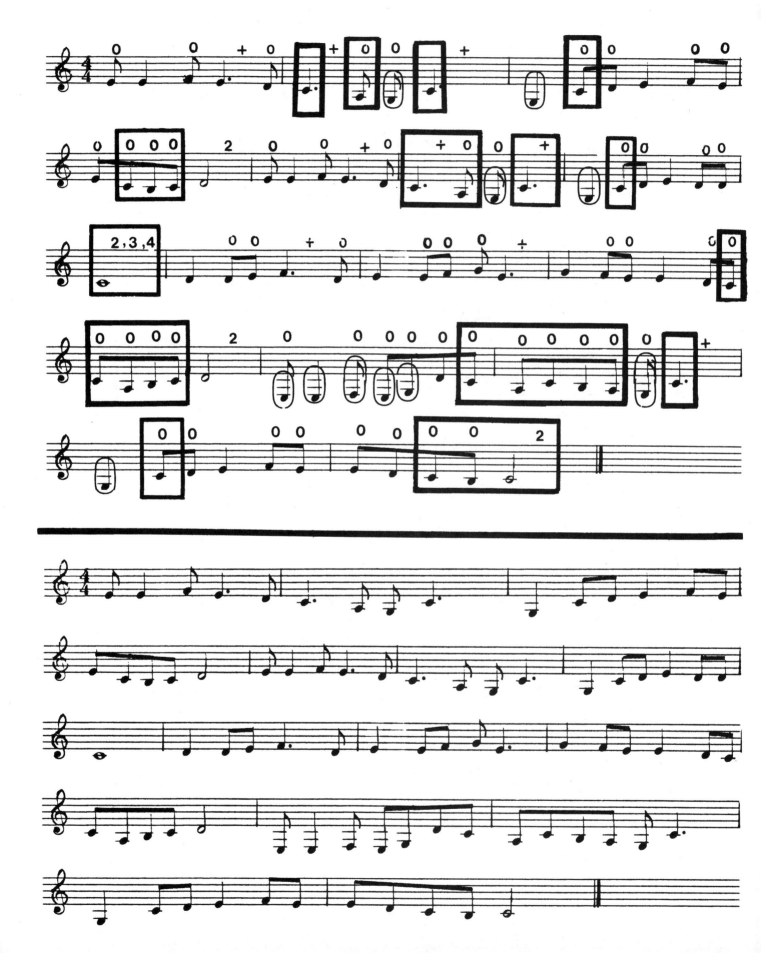

WHILE STROLLING THROUGH THE PARK

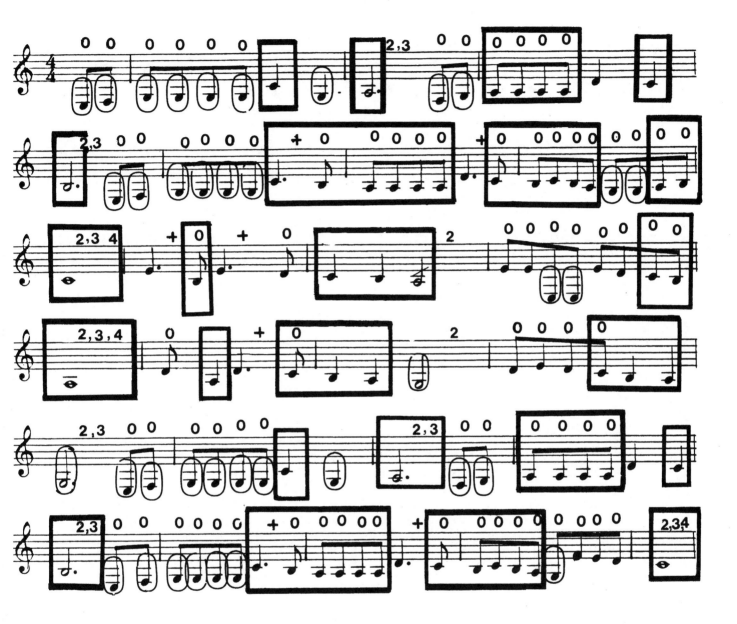

120

WHILE STROLLING THROUGH THE PARK

OUR LAST CHORD

1) We are now ready to try the most difficult of chords for the beginner. The chord we will attempt is called a bar chord. It is called a bar chord because you must press down more than one string with one finger.

THE F CHORD

The bar chord we will learn is F.
To play **F** you put your **1st finger** on the **1st fret** of the **1st string** and on the **1st fret** of the **2nd string**. Put your **2nd finger** on the **2nd fret** of the **3rd string**. Put your **3rd finger** on the **3rd fret** of the **4th string**.

CORRECT F   F   INCORRECT F

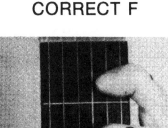 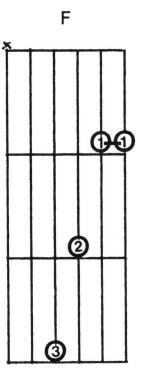 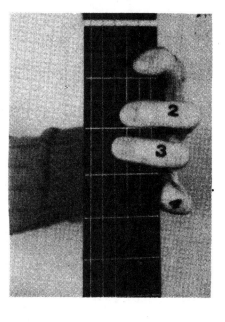

STRINGS WILL SOUND CLEAR

WITH THIS F YOUR 2ND AND 3RD FINGERS ARE BENT OVER TOUCHING OTHER STRINGS AND CAUSING THUDS.

Playing F correctly takes most people a great deal of time. When you push your 1st finger down it causes your 2nd and 3rd finger to bend causing thuds. The only remedy is a great deal of practice. **Put up with the thuds for awhile. They should correct themselves.**

MY BONNIE

C→   F→   C→   F→
My Bon-nie lies o-ver the o-cean,   My Bon-nie lies o-ver the

G⁷→   C→   F→   C→   F→
sea;   My Bon-nie lies o-ver the o-cean,   Oh, bring back my

G⁷→   C→   F→   G⁷→
Bon-nie to me.   Bring back,   bring back,   bring back my

      C→   F→
Bon-nie to me, to me;   Bring back,   bring back,   Oh,

G⁷→   C→
bring back my Bon-nie to me.

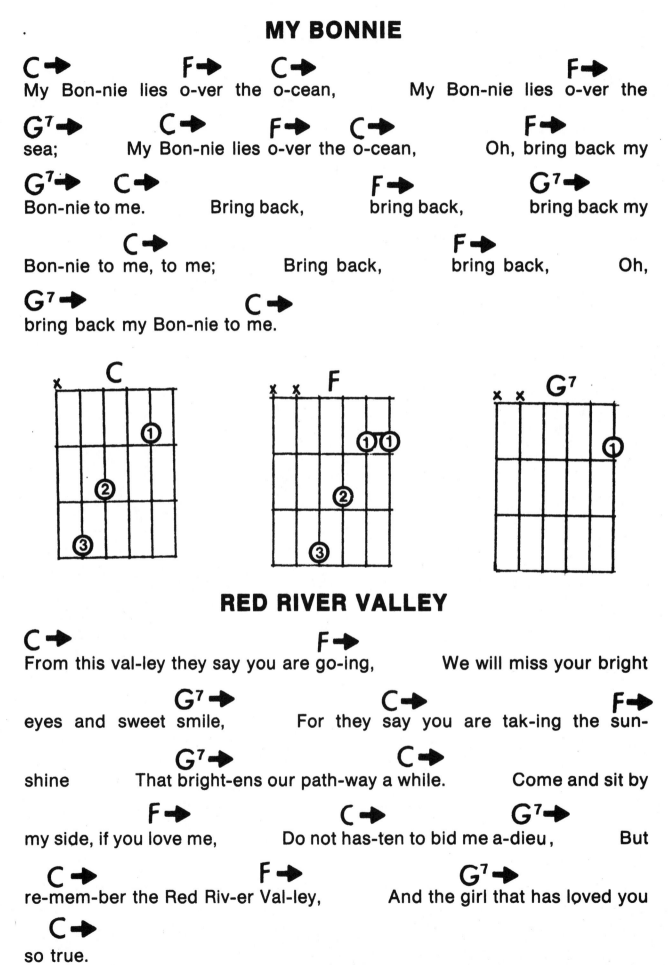

RED RIVER VALLEY

C→   F→
From this val-ley they say you are go-ing,   We will miss your bright

       G⁷→   C→   F→
eyes and sweet smile,   For they say you are tak-ing the sun-

      G⁷→   C→
shine   That bright-ens our path-way a while.   Come and sit by

     F→   C→   G⁷→
my side, if you love me,   Do not has-ten to bid me a-dieu,   But

C→   F→   G⁷→
re-mem-ber the Red Riv-er Val-ley,   And the girl that has loved you

C→
so true.

SILENT NIGHT

C →
Si-lent night!　　　Ho-ly night!　　　G → 　C →
　　　　　　　　　　　　　　　　　All is calm, all is bright

F → 　　　　　　　C → 　　　　F → 　　　C →
Round yon Vir-gin Moth-er and Child! Ho-ly In-fant, so ten-der and mild,

G⁷ → 　　　　　　　C → 　　　G⁷ → 　　　C →
Sleep in heav-en-ly peace,　　　Sleep in heav-en-ly peace.

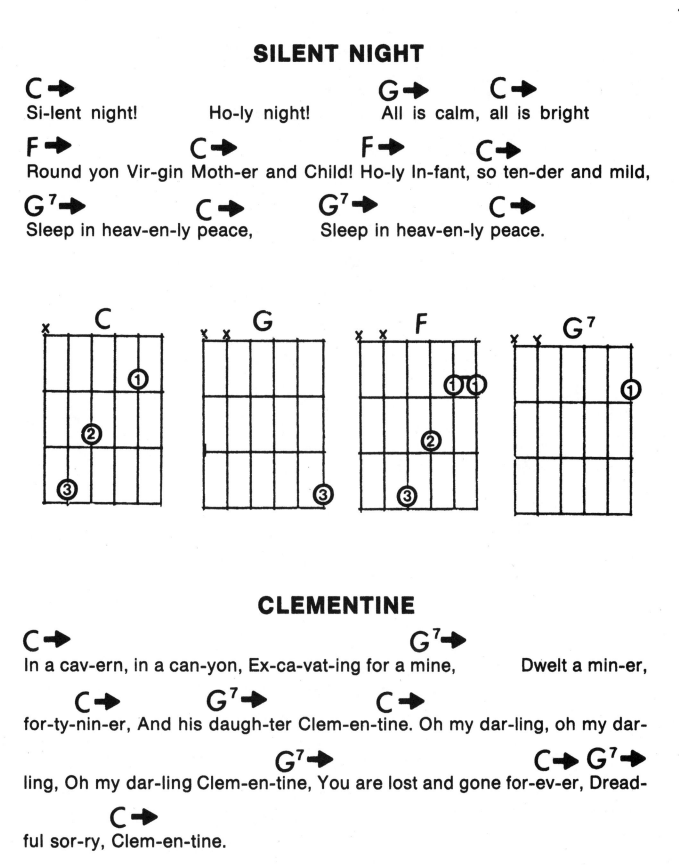

CLEMENTINE

C →　　　　　　　　　　　　　　　　　　　G⁷ →
In a cav-ern, in a can-yon, Ex-ca-vat-ing for a mine,　　　Dwelt a min-er,

　　　　C → 　　　G⁷ → 　　　C →
for-ty-nin-er, And his daugh-ter Clem-en-tine. Oh my dar-ling, oh my dar-

　　　　　　　　　　　G⁷ → 　　　　　　　　　　　C → G⁷ →
ling, Oh my dar-ling Clem-en-tine, You are lost and gone for-ev-er, Dread-

　　　　C →
ful sor-ry, Clem-en-tine.

LITTLE BROWN JUG

C➡   F➡   G⁷➡   C➡

My wife and I lived all a-lone, In a lit-tle log hut we called our own, She loved

F➡   G⁷➡   C➡

gin and I loved rum, I tell you we had lots of fun.   Ha! ha! ha!

F➡   G⁷➡   C➡

you and me   "Lit-tle Brown Jug" don't I love Thee!   Ha! ha!

F➡   G⁷➡   C➡

ha!   you and me   "Lit-tle Brown Jug" don't I love Thee!

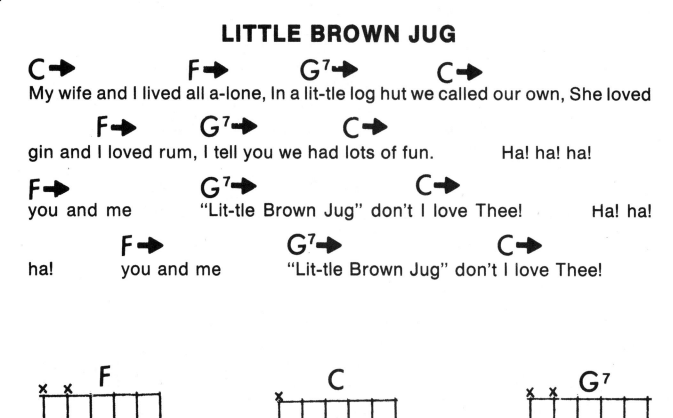

YANKEE DOODLE

C➡   F➡

Yan-kee doo-dle went to town a-rid-ing on a pon-y, he stuck a feath-er in

G⁷➡   C➡ F➡   C➡

his cap and called it mac-a-ro-ni. Yan-kee Doo-dle keep it up, Yan-kee

F➡   G⁷➡   C➡

Doo-dle Dan-dy, Mind the mu-sic and the step and with the girls be han-dy.

DIXIE

C →
I   wish I was   **F →** in de land ob cot-ton, Old times dar am not for-

C →
got-ten, Look a-way! look a-way! look a-way! **G⁷ →** **C →** Dix-ie land,   In

F →
Dix-ie land whar I was born in, Ear-ly on one frost-y morn-in, Look a-

C →
way!   Look a-way!   **G⁷ →** **C →** look a-way! Dix-ie land.   Den I wish

F →   **D⁷ →**   **G⁷ →**   **C →**
I was in Dix-ie,   Hoo-ray,   Hoo-ray!   In Dix-ie land I'll

F →   **C →**   **G⁷ →**   **C →**   **G⁷ →**
take my stand to lib and die in Dix-ie,   A-way,   a-way,

C →   **G⁷ →** **C →**
a-way down south in Dix-ie,   A-way,   a-way,   a-way

down south in Dix-ie.

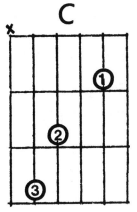
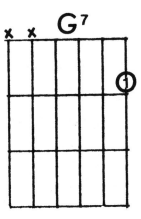
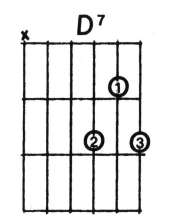
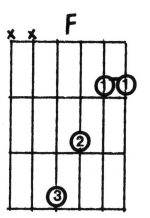

GOODNIGHT, LADIES

C→
Good-night,　　　la-dies,

G⁷→
Good-night, la-dies,

C→　　　　F→
Good-night, la-dies,

C→　G⁷→　C→
We're goin' to leave you now,

C→
Mer-ri-ly we roll a-long,

G⁷→
roll a-long,

C→
roll a-long,

C→
Mer-ri-ly we roll a-long,

G⁷→
o'er the deep blue sea.

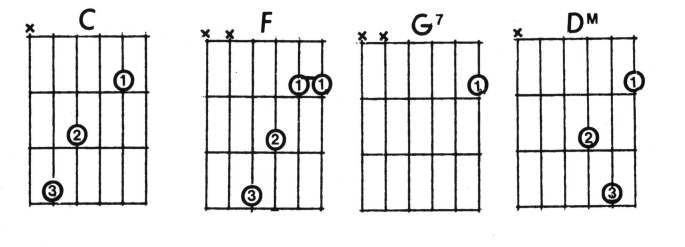

WE WISH YOU A MERRY CHRISTMAS

C→　　　　　　F→　　　　Dᴹ →　　　　G⁷ →
We wish you a Mer-ry Christ-mas, we wish you a Mer-ry Christ-mas, we

C→　　　　　F →　　　　　　　　　G⁷ C→
wish you a Mer-ry Christ-mas, and a Hap-py New Year.

SHARPS

GENERAL RULES

1) This is a sharp sign #

2) When you see this sign you must do something to the note it affects.

3) The sharp sign will appear in two different ways on the music.
   A. The sharp sign always appears on the left of the note it affects. Once a sharp sign appears in front of a note you must sharp the rest of the notes in that measure with the same name.

EXAMPLE

This A would be sharp because it is in the same measure.

This A would be natural because it is in the next measure.

   B. The sharp sign may also appear in the key signature or the very beginning of a song.

As you can see, the sharp sign is on the F line of the staff. This means that ALL F's in this song would be sharp.

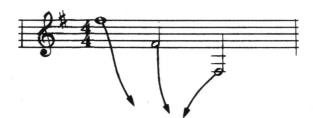

All three of these F's would be sharp.

SHARPS ♯

NUMBER 1

1) In song number 1 all F's would be sharp because the sharp sign is on the F line of the staff. Also, in this song, all C's would be sharp because the sharp sign is on the C space of the staff. **Remember the only notes that are affected in this song would be F and C. All other notes would be played in their regular or natural way.** A song does not have to have sharp signs in the beginning, but it may.

NUMBER 2

2) In song number 2 all C's would be sharp because the sharp sign is on the C space. Also, in this song, all G's would be sharp because the sharp sign is on the G space. ALL F's would be sharp because the sharp sign is on the F line.

3) **Before you play any song you should check for sharp signs. If a note is supposed to be sharp and you don't sharp it, the tune will sound incorrect.**

HOW TO SHARP A NOTE

GENERAL RULE

1) To sharp a note on the guitar you move the note down one fret (towards the hole of your guitar) and remain on the same string. (examples follow) The position of the natural note will be enclosed in a circle and the sharped note in a rectangle.

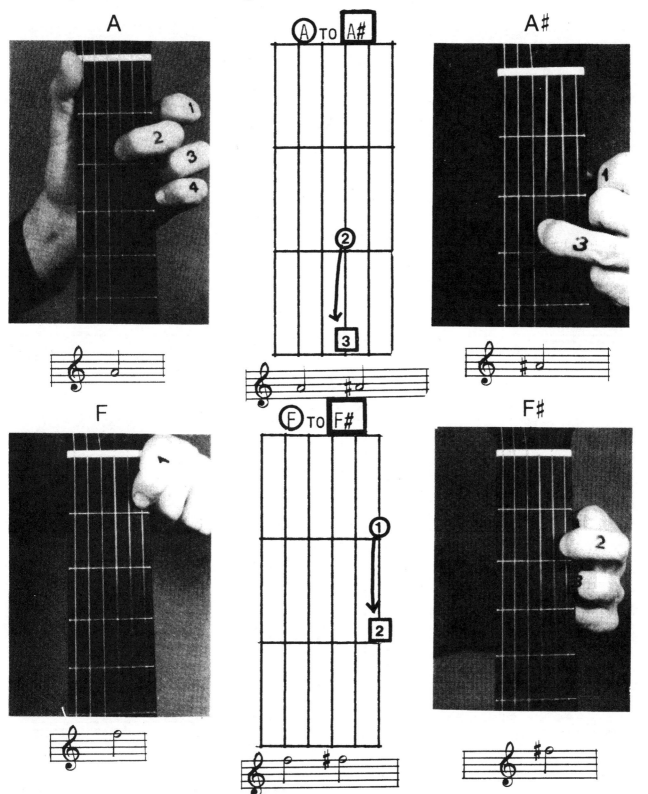

HOW TO SHARP AN OPEN STRING

GENERAL RULE

To sharp an open string you play the 1st fret of the string that is to be sharped (examples follow). The position of the sharped note will be enclosed in a circle.

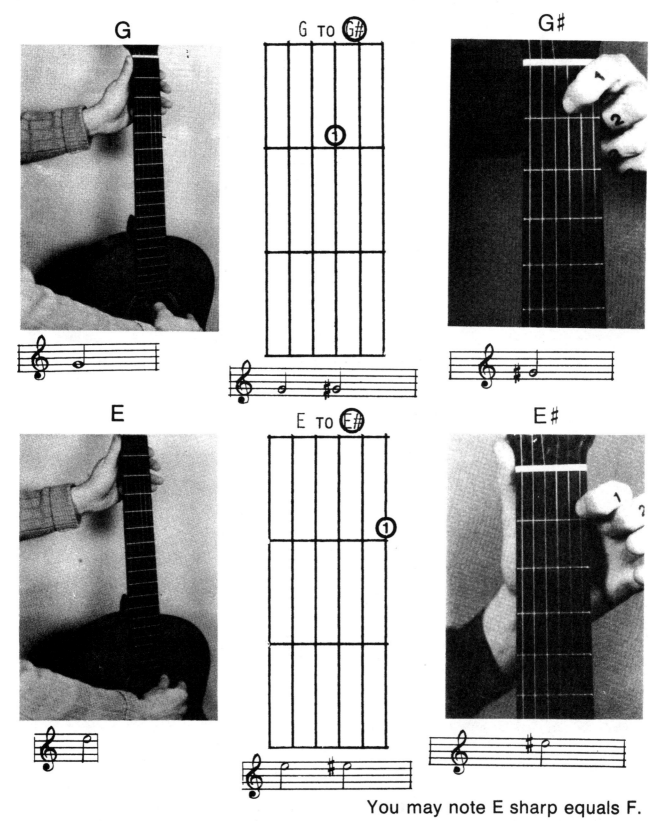

You may note E sharp equals F.

THE NATURAL SIGN ♮

The natural sign removes the sharp from a note.

EXAMPLE 1

This F would also
be natural because it is
in the same measure.

This F would
be natural.

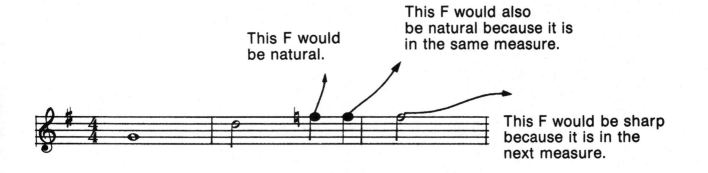

This F would be sharp
because it is in the
next measure.

In this piece of music F's would be sharp. The F that has the natural sign would be played on the 1st fret, 1st string, just like a regular F. The F that follows in the next measure would be sharp again. **The natural sign removes the sharp from that one particular F and all other F's in that measure, if there are any.**

EXAMPLE 2

In this example C was made sharp. The rest of the C's that follow in that measure would also be sharp. Once the natural sign is placed on the C, the remainder of the C's in that measure would be ordinary C (1st finger, 1st fret of the 2nd string) unless another sharp sign is placed down.

THE BAND PLAYED ON

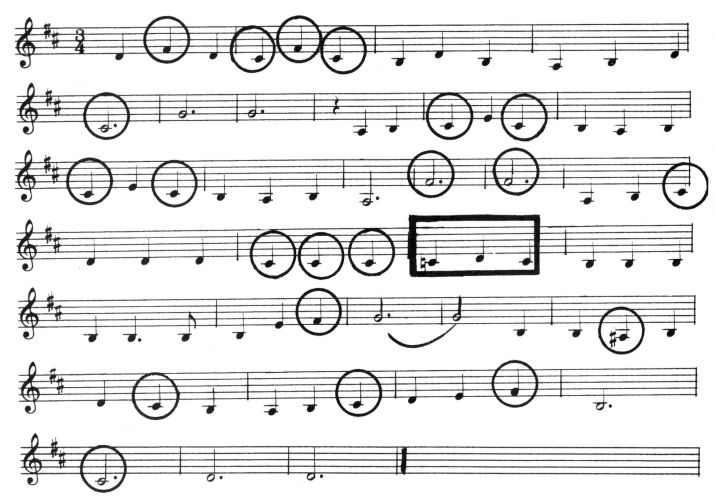

In this song there are two sharps in the key signature.

All F's and C's would be sharped. **In this song and the songs that follow all sharps will be placed in circles.**

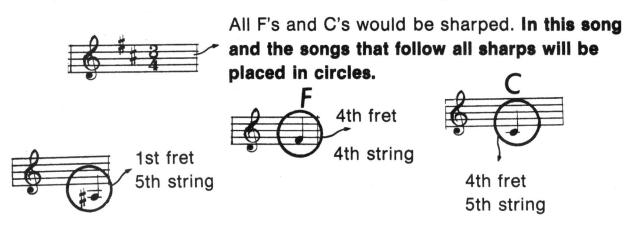

F
4th fret
4th string

C
4th fret
5th string

1st fret
5th string

The natural sign takes the sharp away from this C and the next C in the measure. In the next measure the C's become sharp again.

AFTER THE BALL IS OVER

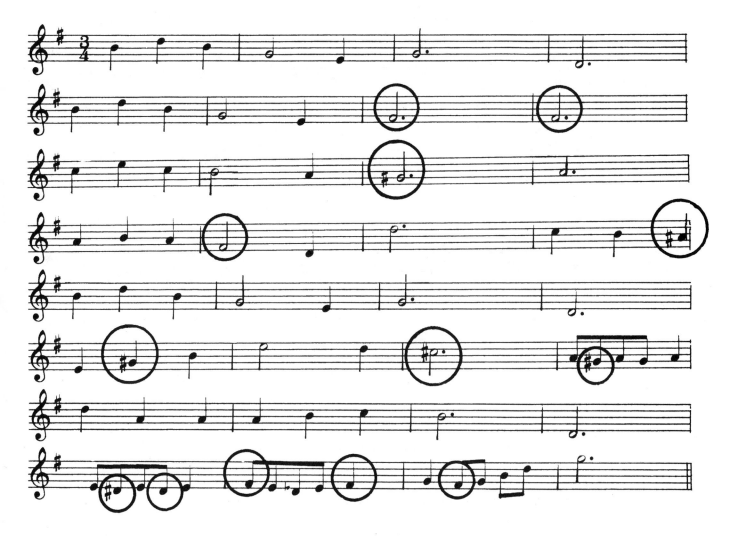

Because of the sharp sign in the key signature all F's in this song are sharp.

4th finger
4th fret
4th string

1st fret
3rd string

3rd fret
3rd string

2nd fret
2nd string

1st fret
4th string

GIVE ME THAT OLD TIME RELIGION

In this song there is a sharp sign in the key signature.

All F's in this song would be sharp because the sharp sign is on the F line of the staff. The two Fs in the song have been circled and would be played 4th finger of the 4th fret of the 4th string.

BEAUTIFUL DREAMER

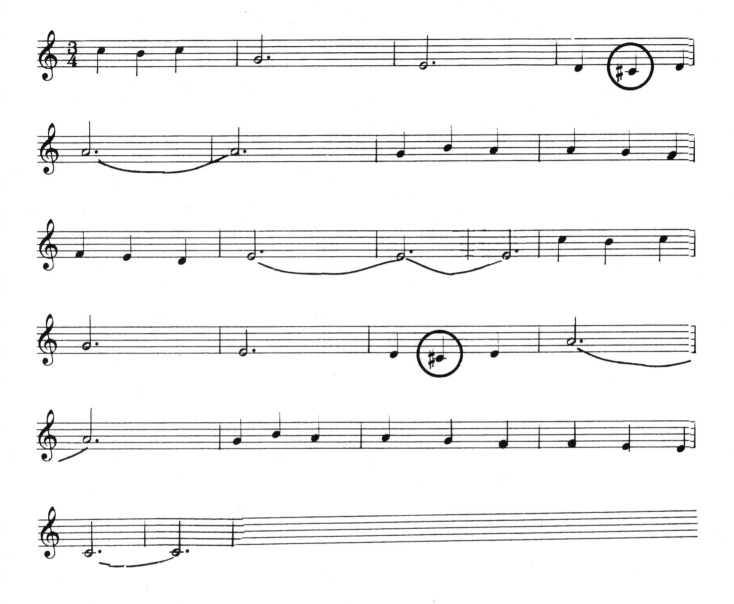

In this song there is not any sharp sign in the key signature or beginning of the song. There are two notes which must be sharped.

Key signature

They are both marked with individual sharp signs. Both of these sharps are the same and should be played on the 4th fret of the 5th string. The regular C would be on the 3rd fret, so to make it sharp you move it down a fret and stay on the same string.

FLATS ♭

GENERAL RULES

1) This is a flat sign ♭

2) When you see this sign you must do something to the note it affects.

3) The flat sign will appear in two different ways on the music.

   A. The flat sign always appears on the left of the note it affects. **Once a flat sign appears on a note you must flat that note and the rest of the notes in that measure.**

EXAMPLE

This A would be flat.

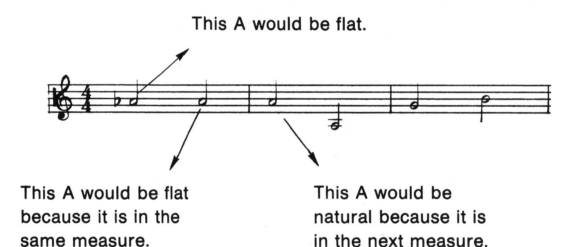

This A would be flat because it is in the same measure.

This A would be natural because it is in the next measure.

STUDENT'S NOTES

FLATS

B. The flat sign may also appear in the key signature or the very beginning of the song.

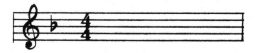

4) As you can see the flat sign is on the B line of the staff. This means that all B's in this song will be flat. All other notes would be played in their regular or natural way.

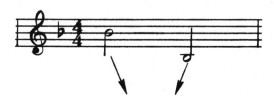

Both of these B's, as well
as any other B in this song,
would have to be flat.

5) In this piece all E's would be flat and all B's would be flat. The flat sign is on the E space of the staff and is also on the B line of the staff. The only notes in this song that would be affected are E's and B's.

HOW TO FLAT A NOTE

GENERAL RULE

To flat a note on the guitar you must move the note up one fret (towards the top of the guitar) and stay on the same string. (examples follow) The position of the natural notes will be enclosed in a circle and the flated notes in a rectangle.

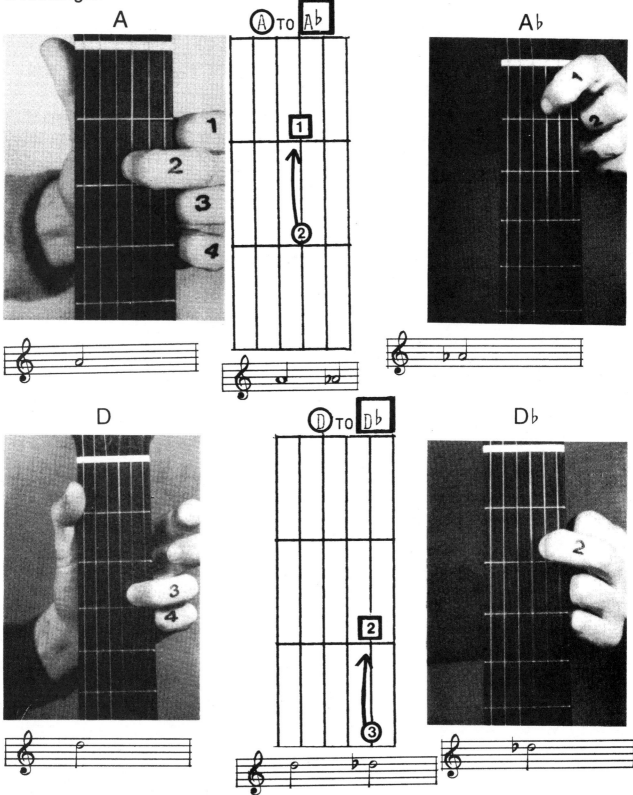

HOW TO FLAT AN OPEN STRING

GENERAL RULE

To flat an open string you move to the next string and play the 4th fret. If the 1st string is flat you would go to the 2nd string. If the second string is flat you would go to the 3rd string etc. . The position of the flats will be enclosed in rectangles. (examples follow)

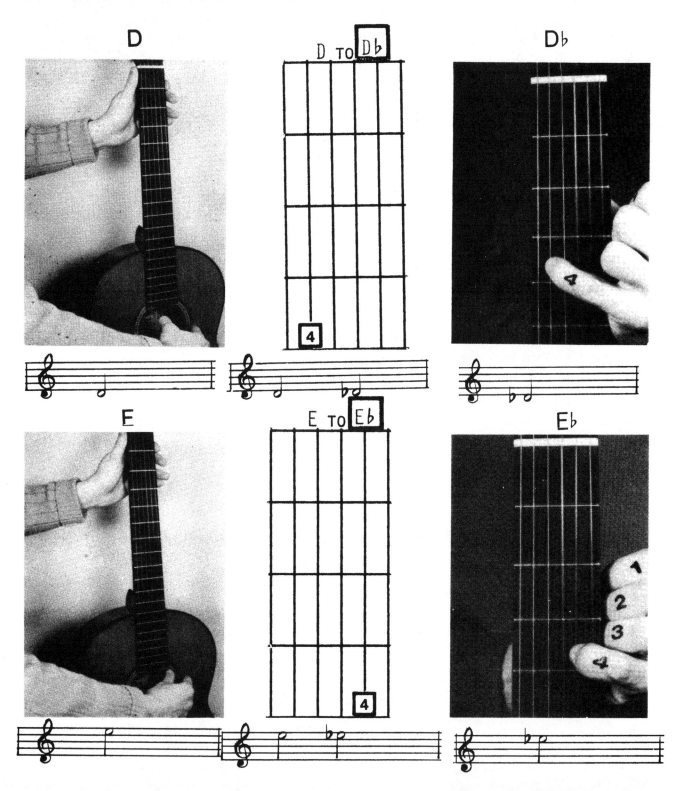

FLATS — EXCEPTIONS TO THE RULES

EXCEPTION 1

B   B TO B♭   B♭

As you can see, the open B is moved to the next string 3rd fret, rather than the 4th fret like the other open strings.

EXCEPTION 2

F and C and F are on the 1st frets. So to flat them you must play that string open.

EXCEPTION 3

is not really an exception —
but you cannot play this note
on your guitar — it is out of range.

THE NATURAL SIGN AGAIN

1) The natural sign removes the flat from a note.

EXAMPLE 1

This B would be natural.

This B would be natural.
because it is in the same measure.

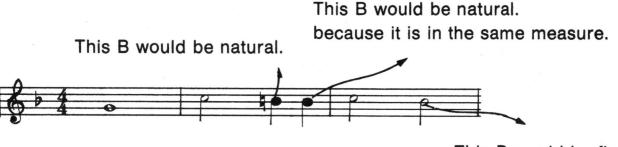

This B would be flat.

In this piece of music all B's would be flat. The exception would be the B that has the natural sign. This B would be played like a regular B (2nd string open). The B that follows in the same measure would also be natural. The B that follows in the next measure should be made flat again.

EXAMPLE 2

In this example A was made flat and the rest of the A's that follow in that measure would also have to be made flat. Once the natural sign is placed on the A, the remainder of the A's in that measure would be regular A. (2nd finger, 2nd fret, 3rd string)

CLEMENTINE

5) Because of the flat sign in the key signature all B's in this song are flat. The flat sign is on the B line of the staff.

3rd fret
3rd string

SWANEE RIVER

There are two flats in the key signature. The two flats in this song are B and E. The flats are placed on the B line of the staff and the E space of the staff. This is how to play the flats in the song in the order they appear.

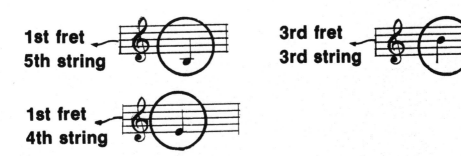

1st fret
5th string

3rd fret
3rd string

1st fret
4th string

ACCOMPANIMENT

1) So far we have learned how to play the melody (notes) by itself, and to play the rhythm (chords) by itself.

2) We will learn how two persons playing the guitar (one notes and the other chords) can accompany each other. We also will learn how a guitarist playing the chords can accompany any other instrument (piano, saxaphone, etc.).

TWO PERSONS PLAYING GUITAR

A) The person playing the notes.

1) The notes are played in the regular manner as you have learned.

2) Instead of counting the notes (one beat after a half-note, 3 beats after a whole-note) the chords will keep time.

3) Instead of counting one after a half-note, you would wait for one strum (one down strum equals one beat). If you have to wait 3 beats (after a whole-note), you would wait 3 strums. In this manner the chords and notes would stay together.

STUDENT'S NOTES

TWO PERSONS PLAYING THE GUITAR

4) Strums

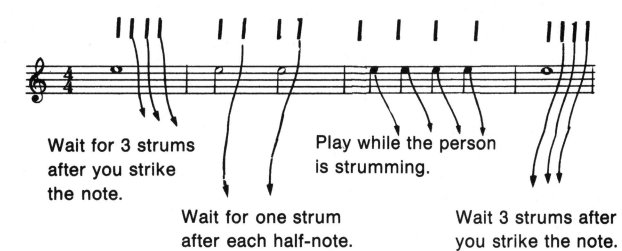

Wait for 3 strums after you strike the note.

Wait for one strum after each half-note.

Play while the person is strumming.

Wait 3 strums after you strike the note.

5) **You can see that the person strums the chord while the person is playing the note and after the person plays the notes.** The person playing the chords plays 4 beats per measure. The quarter notes and other notes will fall in place.

B) The person playing the chords.

1) The person playing the chords is playing straight down strums. The chords must be played at an even and regular pace.

2) How does the person playing the chords know how many times to play each chord per measure?

STUDENT'S NOTES

TWO PERSONS PLAYING THE GUITAR

3) You must look at the time signature to find out how many times to strum the chord per measure. The important number is the top number.

This song would be played 4 strums (or beats) per measure.

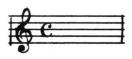

This equals  so it would be played 4 strums per measure.

This would be played 3 strums (or beats) per measure.

This would be played 2 strums (or beats) per measure.

PLAYING THE GUITAR WITH ANOTHER INSTRUMENT

1) Usually, when a person plays the guitar with another instrument the guitarist plays the chords (rhythm).

2) You must tune to the other instrument. Play the high E on that instrument and then tune your 1st string to that E. Then hit the B on the other instrument and tune your second string to that note. Continue this for all six strings and you will be in tune to the other instrument.

3) Look at the time signature and play the number of strums per measure that are necessary. The same rules would be followed here as the rules for accompaning another guitarist. The person playing the other instrument would be playing the notes or the melody. Play the chords as many times as indicated in the time signature.

ALTERNATE STRUMMING

1) So far we have played straight down strums.

2) The guitar chords often sound better if the chords are struck in a down-up fashion.

3) The symbol for a down strum is ⊓ . The symbol for an up strum is V

4) Down—up strums should be played with a pick.

5) As we have seen a down—strum stands for one beat. An up—strum can also stand for one beat.

6) If you are required by the time signature to play 4 beats per measure, you do not have to play 4 strums as long as you play 4 beats.

7) A ⊓V down—up strum is played faster and is equal to one beat. A V V up—up strum is also played faster and is equal to one beat.

8)

⊓ ⊓ ⊓ ⊓ = ⊓ ⊓V ⊓ ⊓V

⊓ ⊓ ⊓ ⊓ = ⊓ ⊓ VV ⊓ | ⊓ ⊓ ⊓ = ⊓ ⊓V ⊓

As you can see, a ⊓V or an V V has been substituted for a down beat.

9) If the time signature says you must play 4 beats per measure, you may play ⊓ ⊓ V V ⊓ rather than ⊓ ⊓ ⊓ ⊓ per measure. You may also play ⊓ ⊓V ⊓ ⊓V per measure. Once you start a song with a strum, you should continue through the entire song with the same strum.

10) If there are two chords in the same measure, and there are 4 beats per measure you could play the 1st chord ⊓ ⊓ and the second chord ⊓ ⊓ . This way there would be a total of 4 beats per measure.

Listen To Side Two B Of Your Record

CHORD ACCOMPANIMENTS

The chords are provided below the titles of the songs in the order that they are played.

O, Dear, What Can The Matter Be...
C G⁷ C G⁷ C

Pop Goes The Weasel..
C G⁷ C G⁷ C G⁷ C G⁷ C

Here We Go Round The Mulberry Bush...
C G⁷ C G⁷ C

A-Tisket A-Tasket...
C G⁷ C G⁷ C

On Top Of Old Smoky...
G C G D⁷ G C G D⁷ G

When The Saints Go Marching In...
C G C F C G C

Jingle Bells...
C F C D⁷ G G⁷ C F C G C

Red River Valley...
C G⁷ C F C G C

Aura Lee...
C D G⁷ C D G⁷ C E F C D F G C

Daisy, Daisy ....
C F C G C D⁷ G C F C G C G C G C

Good Night Ladies...
C G C F C G C G C G C G C F C G C

Silent Night...
C G C F C F C G⁷ C G C

When Johnny Comes Marching Home..
Am C Am C E⁷ Am E⁷ Am E⁷ Am

My Bonnie...
C F C F G C F C F G C F G C F G C

Tom Dooley..
G D G D G

Auld Lang Syne...
G D G C G D C G D G C G D C D G

Oh Susanna...
G D⁷ G D G D⁷ G D G C G D G D G

Blow The Man Down..
C G⁷ C

Michael Row The Boat Ashore..

    C F C Am F G C F C Am F C G C G C

Shoo Fly, Don't Bother Me...

    C G C G C G C G C

The Yellow Rose Of Texas...

    C G^7 C Am Dm G^7 C G C

Joshua Fit The Battle Of Jericho..

    Am E^7 Am E^7 ....

Scarborough Fair..

    Am G Am C Am C E Am C G E Am G Am

Camptown Races...

    G D^7 G D^7 G C G D^7 G

Long Long Ago...

    G D^7 G D^7 G D^7 G D^7 G D^7 G

My Old Kentucky Home...

    C F C Am D^7 G^7 C F C G^7 C F C C^7 F C F C G^7 C

Londonderry Air..

    C F C G C F G C F C Am F C G^7 C F C G C

I've Been Working On The Railroad...

    C F C D^7 G C C^7 F E^7 F C G^7 C

Carry Me Back To Old Virginny...

    C C^7 F C D^7 G C C^7 F C G^7 C G C D^7 C F C A^7 D^7 C

While Strolling Through The Park..

    C F D^7 G C F D^7 G^7 C E^7 Am E^7 A D^7 G D^7 G^7 C F D^7 G^7 C F D^7

G^7 C

The Band Played On..

    D A^7 D A D^7 G Em G D E^7 A^7 D

After the Ball Is Over...

    G C G D^7 Am E^7 Am D^7 G D^7 G C G E^7 A^7 G A^7 D^7 G

Give Me That Old Time Religion...

    G D G C G D^7 G D^7 G

Beautiful Dreamer...

    C Dm G^7 C G C Dm G^7 C

Clementine..

    F C^7 F C^7 F C^7 F C^7 F

Swanee River...

    Bb Eb F^7 Bb Eb Bb F^7 Bb F^7 Bb Eb F^7 Bb Eb Bb F^7 Bb

STUDENT NOTES